Living Longer
and Other
Sobering Possibilities

by

Tom Mullen

Merry Christmas 1997

I know you like Tom Mullen + his thoughts on life are inspiring. This book is NOT about us, but about those we love!

Love
Becky

Written Permission must be secured from the publisher to
use or reproduce any part of this book, except for brief quotations in critical
reviews or articles.

Printed in the United States of America
Friends United Press
101 Quaker Hill Drive
Richmond, IN 47374

Library of Congress Cataloging-in-Publication Data

Mullen, Thomas James, 1934-
Living Longer and other Sobering Possibilities / Tom Mullen.
        p.   cm.
ISBN 0-944350-39-9
1. Wit and humor-- Religious aspects--Christianity. 2. Aged-Religious life.
I. Title.
BR115.H84M85 1996
248.8'5--dc20   96-14674
                                                            CIP

Cover design by Kathy Kline Miller

To Sam and Ruth Neff
Close friends, excellent Friends

Contents

Foreword

I first heard Tom Mullen speak when he was a guest lecturer for a large gathering of United Methodist women in a hotel ballroom in St. Paul, Minnesota. I was fascinated by the way he could hold their attention, drive home his salient points, and move them alternately to laugh or cry over some shared memory. Three years later, when I was responsible for the religious programming at a summer Chautauqua, Tom was one of the first speakers I invited to preach and lecture. Over a period of seven summers, I have been privileged to have some of the best known names in American religion as guest speakers. On three different occasions Tom has come and given leadership for an entire week. He always draws the largest response. The lectures compete with other summer activities: tennis, golf, the beach, shopping and cultural events. It requires, with all those options, an enormously popular speaker to necessitate setting up additional chairs. (I have defined the Methodist version of heaven as "Chairs in the aisle.)" But every time Tom has been the guest speaker, attendance has exceeded seating capacity. I have often said there are preachers who effectively use humor. Tom is a humorist who is also an effective preacher.

Quaker theologian Elton Trueblood, who greatly influenced Tom Mullen, published a book on *The Humor of Christ* (1964) and describes thirty-one instances where Christ uses humor. The Bible reminds us that joy is the one infallible sign of the presence of God. "Do not be grieved for the joy of the Lord is your strength." (Nehemiah 8:10) Someone has put it this way: "Laughter is the rainbow that arches the tears of humanity."

Shortly after receiving the manuscript, with a request to write a foreword, my wife and I were taking a trip, so I read it to her while she was driving. Again and again, we found ourselves laughing as we came to some witty observation. In describing the book to a colleague at the seminary where I now teach, I said: "It's a 'fun read.' It doesn't seem profound but suddenly you realize it is."

Tom discusses conducting a workshop for a group of caregivers to Alzheimer's patients. He writes: "During the workshop we explored ways humor and laughter enable us to keep life's trials in perspective. The group embraced the idea as if they had been seeking permission to laugh as an antidote to the pain and stress of daily care giving..." In reading the book I had the sense that Tom was also giving himself permission to laugh as an antidote to the frustrating illnesses he and Nancy have experienced.

It's a book about growing older, and since anyone able to read is still here and thus growing older, it has interest for all of us. Its primary audience, however, are those of us who are moving through and beyond the mid-years.

It covers a wide range of topics: hospitalizations, relating to your adult children, grand-parenting, utilizing spiritual resources during the aging process, handling retirement, and preparing for your own funeral.

I am older than Tom and Nancy, so I can relate to all the experiences he describes. I, too, grew up in a devout home in mid-America. I am, after fifty-three years of married life, still in love with the woman with whom I shared vows. We, too, have reared four children and we relate to nine grandchildren. On our fiftieth wedding anniversary, we took our children, and their spouses, (plus the older grandchildren) on a cruise, so I identify with his description of the trip he and Nancy enjoyed in Hawaii.

Not only am I older, but I am further along in my journey than Tom and Nancy. I retired from the active episcopacy of the United Methodist Church in 1988, and adjusted by finding new and useful ways of using my time even while enjoying more flexibility of schedule. My wife often says I receive many job offers because I come cheap! In addition to my summer work, I teach part-time at a seminary (and during the 1995-96 academic year served as Acting

President); I am "Bishop in Residence" at a church. I often tell my friends: "There is life after retirement."

Life has chapters. Each has its reward, fulfillment, and challenge. I have enjoyed my post-retirement phase as much as any of the previous ones when I was a college teacher, a pastor, and a bishop. My wife and I were married the year I graduated from college. We were young. Our first child was born a year later. We often say we " grew up together." Our four children, however, are five or six years apart in age. The advantage was we only had one in college at a time. The disadvantage was we belonged to the PTA for thirty-two years! I made my last tuition payment the year I retired. After so many years of parenting, we were ready for the "empty nest stage."

In contrast to Tom and Nancy's major and critical health problems, I was seventy-three before I had my first hospital experience. It came shortly after I heard Tom give the essence of this book in a series of lectures. In reading the manuscript, I found myself relating [as can many of you] to his description of a hospital stay. The humor, of course, does not conceal the fact that it is often painful, frequently frightening, but also has moments of reassurance and grace when you find personnel thoughtful, sensitive, and caring as well as professionally skilled.

Tom is realistic in acknowledging there are no easy answers to the question of "Why?" The book of Job struggles with this question and offers no facile conclusion. I remember standing by the hospital bed of a parishioner who began the conversation by asking: "What have I done that this should happen to me?" I answered, "You probably haven't done anything except join the human race." Most of us, if we stay here very long, will have health problems, suffer some family disappointments, and see at least a few of our hopes frustrated.

I commend this slender volume to you with the hope that as you journey your pilgrimage, you will find it rich with insights you have discovered but not yet put into words; that it will strengthen your faith, equipping you to see God's hand in the affairs of your life, and that it will enhance your ability not only to cope with but find joy in life's mysteries, complexities, and adventures.

Emerson S. Colaw
A bishop of the United Methodist Church (retired)
Dayton, Ohio

Preface

This book is a collection of essays about growing older. They are reflections about one person's life and consequently are haphazard. They do not come close to saying all that is worth saying about aging, but they examine my perceptions about life between fifty-six and sixty-one, the time during which I finally realized I was old.

In a way this book is a sequel to *Middle Age and Other Mixed Blessings* which was published in 1991. Since that book appeared, we've added two grandchildren, survived life-threatening illnesses, experienced the amputation of my wife's leg, and begun semi-retirement from Earlham School of Religion.

Because my experience in growing older is limited to myself and my wife, the book is incomplete. I wonder: Can others connect their experience to my own? And will I look back ten years from now and see things entirely differently?

In the face of these questions, two realities persuaded me to write this book now in spite of inherent limitations. First, writing close to events serves to keep the passion and insights associated with the experience fresh and alive. Yes, the future may cause us to reconsider, but some lessons are learned right away.

Second, while my experiences are limited by my own human boundaries, in most ways I'm like a real person. My hope is that other real people will be able to identify with these essays and reflect upon their own lives and how the Christian faith speaks to them.

The contents of the book have been tested in several places. Sixteen of the essays appeared in *Quaker Life* over a five-year period. They have been edited to fit into this book, and I hope the good reputation of that magazine has not been damaged by having published what I've written.

During the summer of 1995, I delivered the Shearer Lectures at the Assembly of the Bay View Association near Petoskey, Michigan. That group of wonderful people provided feedback, raised questions, and added insights that have made this book better than it otherwise would have been. Audiences vary as much as speakers, and the Bay View audience is always an inspiring and encouraging one. I'm grateful.

Our adult children gave feedback and made historical corrections of events distorted by their father's selective memory. Sarah Northrop, our oldest daughter, prepared the copy for the publisher and read the manuscript word for word. The other children—Martha, Brett, and Ruth—also heard or read portions of the book and have decided not to file suit.

West Richmond Friends Meeting, the Quaker congregation which has nurtured the Mullen family for over thirty years, has helped shape my theological perspective. Its members demonstrate haphazard theology, too, and liberal, orthodox, and conservative Christianity is present in varying degrees—as it is in this book. The Meeting functions as a caring, supporting, forgiving community, and when a congregation behaves like this, the Living Christ is present and writers of books are nurtured.

Finally, I'm enormously grateful to a long list of persons—friends, students, colleagues at Earlham, relatives in our extended family, and a few people we've known only a short time. Their love and understanding touched Nancy and me deeply as they walked with us through the Valley of the Shadow in the autumn of 1995. Each one deserves our gratitude.

Two persons from that long list must be singled out, both because we share a deep friendship and also because they model what it means to be brothers and sisters in Christ. My wife and I are not the only ones whose lives they have embraced, for Sam and Ruth Neff love humankind in general—Russians, Cubans, Native Americans, and anybody else who is fortunate to be in their path as they walk through life. But their affection for us and their devotion to their own family are exemplary, and Nancy and

I happily dedicate this book to them. Sam and Ruth, you deserve better but this is what we have to give, with our love.

—Tom Mullen

Part I

One Day at a Time

In our fifties, says sociologist David Karp, we become "socialized into illness," no longer blithely assume good health and, instead, view ourselves more and more as patients. We may watch our parents' health decline, and we see their gradual deterioration as a preview of our own coming circumstances.

This has been true in my own case. I became a diabetic at age thirty-five, had my first surgery at forty-five (a hemorrhoidectomy), an operation at age fifty-seven when my colon was removed, and reconstructive surgery at age sixty-one when I acquired Crohn's disease. Several hospital stays made me conscious of my mortality, and health maintenance became a priority.

During my first forty-five years I spent no time in hospitals, and doctors were people I saw annually for a physical examination. Now, in my sixties, each day includes a regimen that takes time and discipline. Both Nancy and I test our blood sugars as often as four times a day. The result of these tests dictates the calories we'll consume and the amount of insulin we'll inject that day.

Each morning at breakfast we take nine different pills. Pills, in fact, provide the main bulk of our diets. Twice a week I change my ileostomy bag, and Nancy and I continually remind each other what to eat—or avoid eating. Two foods that I adored more than any others (popcorn and peanuts) have been removed from my diet, and the digestive problems I have when I violate this restriction seem like a message from God. Health problems and aging are usually kindred phenomena. As catabolism, the process of growing older, takes its toll, our infirmities become more obvious. One pundit said, "If I'd known I was going to live so long, I'd have taken better care of myself." The worst response toward aging is to deny it, to act as if we can do what we used to do. Better to cooperate with the inevitable and ignore the eighty-year-old man in the television commercial who water skis in his bare feet. We can still answer when opportunity knocks, but it takes longer to get to the door.

The essays which follow describe one man's struggle with deteriorating health. They are presented in chronological order because the older Nancy and I became, the more serious, indeed, devastating the effects of disease and diabetes were. But the key lesson that the Christian faith helped us learn as we went through treatments, surgery, and physical loss was this: it is possible to rejoice and give thanks *in* all circumstances.

The preposition is important. It's not easy to give thanks *for* disease or the amputation of a leg. It is possible to rejoice *in the middle* of such circumstances, and laughing as well as crying go together. We learn to live one day at a time, and that day becomes a gift from God.

1

No Pain, No Gain

Minor surgery is what is done to someone else. Major surgery is what happens to you. Twenty-seven days in the hospital and the removal of my colon convinced me of this truth, even though many others were in worse shape than I. Nevertheless, my own pain provided ample opportunity to focus on my private misery and wallow in self-pity.

This was not entirely due to weakness of character, although my ability to transcend pain is less than Rambo's. Hospital routines, however, are designed to feed one's paranoia, and twenty-seven days in a modern hospital are very different from a luxury hotel, even though hospitals cost more.

The hospital staff *always* wants you to do the opposite of what you feel like doing. After surgery, a patient longs to lie as still as possible, moving nary a muscle in the faint hope of keeping those parts of his insides that haven't been removed from falling out. Certain nurses make sure surgical patients are up and walking right after their operations. One's pitiful looks and pathetic whining touches these Florence Nightmare-gales not at all, so up you get and walk you do.

And it hurts. Walking—nay, staggering—down the hall a few hours after your abdomen had been savaged by a wealthy man wearing a mask while you were asleep probably violates your constitutional rights. Thus, wearing a foot-long incision held together by metal staples like those used to install insulation in attics, you lean on your wife's arm and hang weakly on the hallway railing step by painful step. People you meet, who don't have staples in their stomachs, attempt levity. "No running allowed. Ha! Ha!" The nurse urges you on, as she has more patients to torment before she goes to her other job as a marine corps drill instructor.

Completing the walk and returning to one's bed for sleep is the one hope that sustains a patient. After having been sliced and stapled, thumped and pumped, probed and prodded, sleep has been earned. It is deserved. It is a sign of justice in the world.

Sleep, however, is prohibited by hospital routine. Consider my experience. Connected as I was by I.V. tubes to a variety of antibiotics, liquid nutrition, and other fluids clogging my blood vessels, I discovered that each bottle of stuff was timed to run out every half-hour. You know they are depleted each half-hour because a beeper sounds continuously until someone comes and shuts it off. That is usually quite a while because hospital personnel know that beepers do not cause bodily harm, even though the temptation to do so to the nurse by the patient grows in direct proportion to the beeps endured. Changing I.V.'s kept me totally awake between 11:00 p.m. and 1:30 a.m. when the drippings were finally done for the night.

Promptly at 5:00 a.m., however, Count Dracula arrives to get a blood sample. While it is not true that blood removal is the primary form of health care in the United States, hospital personnel continually lunge at you with needles. True, blood is needed to cover maybe two small glass slides in the laboratory, but this does not explain why so much has to be drawn so often.

Blood-takers follow a set routine which is learned in blood-taking school and never varies no matter the age, condition, or I.Q. of the patient. First, a rubber hose is twisted around a patient's arm tight enough to force his vein to stand at attention. Next the target area is cleaned with alcohol. Then a short, silent pause follows in which the patient anxiously anticipates what is to come. The laboratory person then says "stick" while simultaneously plunging into your arm a needle slightly larger than those used to immunize horses. After a pint or so of blood has been drawn, the blood-taker carefully tapes a piece of cotton to the hairiest part of your arm. Then, like the Lone Ranger, he steals away without waiting for thanks—although thanking him is scarcely the first response that comes to mind.

During the brief interlude when blood is *not* being drawn, bags of fluids are *not* being attached to your I.V.'s, and you are *not* being dragged out of bed for the hospital equivalent of the Bataan death march, doctors and others read and write on your chart. Every deed done to you, every vital sign is there recorded, as are any unusual symptoms such as cheerfulness after surgery or fondness for hospital food.

Physicians volunteer almost no information to their patients, even though we may have some curiosity as to whether we will live another day. Instead, they write new orders for nurses to carry out or occasionally look over the top of their eye glasses to murmur "uh huh" or "oh! oh!" Such phrases, unexplained, increase one's faith as the patient quickly wants to get right with God.

Nurses also read a patient's chart in order to complain about the physician's handwriting. "Did he order four units or eight units of prednisone?" Since the larger amount of that drug turns people into werewolves, the patient hopes what is written is what is intended.

Other people stop by to read your chart, too, such as interns who have come to study you due to a shortage of cadavers. LPN's also read your medical history, and they often offer medical opinions. One, for example, looked at my chart and said, "You are one sick puppy!"

So, why, given the unpleasantness of the hospital routine, is this former patient thankful to God for it? Not because it's a perfect routine. It isn't, and some ways of doing things in hospitals make no sense and mistakes in treatment do occur.

Nevertheless, there's no gain without pain. What eventually is good for us evidently has to hurt. I've concluded that trusting the routine is like having faith. Your life is out of your control, so you have to have faith in others. And somehow you have to believe that the end will justify the routine.

And when it does, when that glorious day arrives and you can cart your poor punctured, punished, pummeled body home, finally you can appreciate your hospital stay in a proper perspective—at a distance, without beepers and with a reasonable possibility of a full night's sleep. Amen.

"I know you released him Doctor, but he says
he likes the food and refuses to leave."

2

Thanks, Friends

Why undergo major surgery for a life-threatening condition and then fail to talk and write about it at every opportunity? Over the years I've listened attentively while others have rambled on about their operations. Now that God has given me the occasion to talk about mine, I intend to do so. And I know that people want to hear about *my* surgery. One even said that my talking about colon removal was like a drink of cold water to a drowning man.

Thus, this essay is about the care and support I received as a patient. It was remarkable. I was overwhelmed by cards, letters, phone calls, visits, gifts, and many other expressions of love and concern. In fact, now that I'm feeling and looking well, I have learned to feign a limp so as to elicit cards, letters and—best of all—gifts of food like those which flowed in during my illness. The joy of having someone ask, "How are you?" and expect an answer is a powerful invitation to a conscientious hypochondriac like me to dominate conversations and fill books like this one.

Many nurses and chaplains demonstrated care and concern while I was a patient. Some were more helpful than others. The nurse who regularly asked, "How are *we* feeling today?" caused a dilemma. While I had a good sense of how I felt, I really had no idea how *she* was doing.

Once, a nurse responded to my push on the call button. I had called for help right before I fainted and was crawling, semi-conscious, on all fours trying to figure out how to get back into bed. I admit that the sight of a grown man, crawling about while wearing one of those indecent hospital gowns and connected by two plastic tubes to a large machine that goes "beep" every five seconds is interesting, possibly fascinating. Her question, however, continues to intrigue me, as it did at the time. "May I help you?" she asked. The answer, to me, seemed obvious, and to this day I wish I had been alert enough to have responded, "No, I'm just crawling about at 2:00 a.m. looking for loose change."

Since Methodist Hospital in Indianapolis is a center for Clinical Pastoral Education, many chaplains visited me. Having taught pastoral care at the Earlham School of Religion, I had opportunity to observe their technique and style. Most did very well. One, however, had the unnerving habit of squeezing my big toe while standing at the foot of the bed and praying. What I learned is that having one's toe squeezed and wiggled during prayer does not add to its spiritual power; in fact, it tends to tickle.

Visits by friends from my own congregation and other churches will never be forgotten. They went out of their way to comfort and cheer me. My pastor drove over one hundred fifty miles on the fourth of July to visit me. True, there was an outstanding fireworks display that day which could be enjoyed from the hospital window, but he came to see *me* who could provide no multicolored explosions in the sky.

And I'll remember a long time the note which came from a faculty colleague that said, "It is the sense of the meeting that we want you to get well soon." The next sentence kept my elation under control, for it said, "Two members of the faculty stood aside."

Laughing with friends and loved ones during recovery was as important as praying with them. Laughing is second only to coughing in causing pain after one has had a major incision in his abdomen, but it's worth it. It's a form of intimacy, for we laugh most with the same people with whom we cry. Sometimes we do both, for I laughed until I cried.

The concern and care that a few expressed were particularly helpful because they had been through surgery like mine years before. Because they shared their medical stories, I had to resist the temptation to whine, whimper, and wail in exclamations of self-pity. Letters from two friends revealed that both had had operations like mine, and they both had not only survived but were living their lives with dignity and joy. Like Job, I had complained, "Why me?" Because of the example of these friends, I was forced to answer a different question, "Why not me?"

At Methodist Hospital where I was a patient, a team of nurses works with all of us who have "ostomies"—colostomies, ileostomies (my condition), and similar surgeries that remove or by-pass certain organs. One of the nurses on the team has an ileostomy herself. She acquired it at age twelve, was now in her forties, married, the mother of two children, and worked full-time as a nurse. As we discussed the life-style adjustments that go with an ileostomy, as well as the fears and worries that accompany it, she was both sensitive and straightforward.

On one occasion, I shared my concern about getting a leak in the plastic bag that replaced my colon. What should I do? Her reply: "Always stand downwind!" While I was still savoring that thought, she added: "Besides, women who have an ileostomy have a problem men don't have. Both men and women wear bags, but we women have to find shoes that match."

I laughed so hard my stitches stretched—and they were made of metal. Her comment was more than a clever joke; she demonstrated that human beings can handle a lot of adversity, so we might as well be cheerful about it.

The Apostle Paul said that in the body of Christ, members have the same care for one another. "If one member suffers, all suffer together; if one member is honored, all rejoice together." (I Corinthians 12:26) We're wounded healers and honored rejoicers.

Having major surgery is harder than *talking* about it later, but both are necessary. If we don't talk about it, we lose the chance to be the center of attention among those who innocently ask how we are. More important, if we remain silent, those good folk who cared may not learn how much, how very much, their deeds and words meant to at least one post middle-aged diabetic Quaker who has an ileostomy. He knows he's loved, even when it takes the form of bad jokes and squeezed toes during prayer.

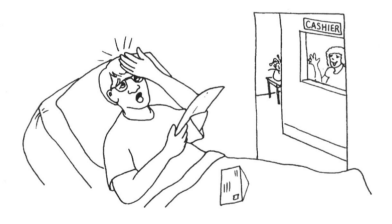

Dear Mr. Mullen.
In order to save postage the hospital has hand delivered your $112,000 bill to your room. Have a pleasant stay.

3

Here's to Our Health!

When I was fifty-eight, I spent Thanksgiving in the hospital for surgery. It was the third operation in two years, and it enabled me to experience Thanksgiving from the point of view of the turkey. Over my first fifty-six years, I was in the hospital a total of six days. In the following four years I was a patient on six different occasions for a total of fifty-two days. While some of you reading these words have logged more hospital time, I still feel called to share my "insider" information about the experience. After all, once we've worn a hospital gown for any length of time, we're ready to reveal what's in our heads, too.

Observation 1: Going to the hospital is expensive. Lying in a hospital bed is like sleeping in a parked taxi while the meter is running. Some hospitals now locate the recovery room next to the cashier's office. One of my roommates was a medicare patient, and he asked the nurse to put a sign on his bed that read "Your Tax Dollars at Work."

Why do the same pills we take at home cost so much more when taken in the hospital? Does the little wad of cotton in the bottle require surgical removal? And the wonder of wonder drugs is their cost. Until I became a patient I was näive about how expensive miracle medicine was. To me quinine and castor oil were miraculous enough, but today's wonder drugs are exotic and have remarkable curative powers. They are also expensive, and one of their side effects is bankruptcy. One pill I was taking for colitis cost so much my prescription said to take it as often as I could afford to do so.

I found that my ability to overcome disease and recover from surgery was directly related to six words: "Your health insurance doesn't cover that." As I began to feel better, my worry about expense became worse. When I was really sick, costs didn't matter. Indeed, next to discovering that hospital food is inedible, worrying about costs is the best evidence we're recovering.

Observation 2: Our relationships with doctors become personal. As we get older, we suspect that nature is plotting against us for the benefit of the medical profession. We ask: Do I really need this surgery, or is the doctor adding a room to his house?

Fortunately, the surgeon who cut on me was so wealthy he occasionally informed patients that surgery was not necessary. He was congenial and delighted in telling me his favorite jokes. They weren't very funny, but he kept me in stitches. I respected his medical skills, and he tolerated my religious and political views. We became friends. It was right that we did, as anyone who removes your colon should be addressed by his first name. Somehow I was comforted in knowing the man behind the mask who cut on my body while I was asleep was a friend.

We need doctors. For the most part, they do far more good than harm. And if there were no doctor's offices, what would we do with old magazines?

Observation 3: Being well is better than being sick or dead. Time spent in the hospital, in surgery, and recuperating is worthwhile if our energy returns and we can be useful once again. As we get older, life seems an ongoing struggle to keep money coming in and teeth, hair, and vital organs from coming out.

Of course, having surgery means we can solicit sympathy from friends, and I have talked much more about my colon since it was removed than I did while it was attached. But even better than talking about my surgery is the fact I'm healthier with an ileostomy than I was with a diseased colon.

Despite all the pain, trouble, and inconvenience, getting well has more appeal than most other options. Nancy and I are both diabetics, and we can be healthy if we eat properly and take our insulin. We can drink sugar-free soda pop and enjoy occasional lo-cal desserts. And because both of us are diabetics, we call each other nutra-sweetheart. Even love can be sugar free!

No one wants to be ill or looks forward to surgery, even though indulgent lifestyles and bad eating habits will bring many of us to hospitals sooner or later. As I look back on the pain and trouble my health problems caused, I would have preferred to skip the whole ordeal. And if given the choice, I will always choose a night in the Hilton over a night in the hospital—and not just because it's cheaper.

Nevertheless, if I'm not particularly grateful for what happened to me, I'm very thankful for what I escaped. Medical care —pain and all—is a gift from God.

Yes, it's expensive. Yes, some doctors are so wrapped up in their specialties we have to change physicians when a cold moves from our nose to our chest. Yes, hospitals have mysterious procedures and unfathomable bureaucracies that keep health costs high. And, yes, we patients bring our own bundles of insecurities and self-pity when we seek medical help.

The reason for seeking good health, however, is to live a useful life. Whether sick or healthy, we still live by the Grace of God. And those rich people in white coats and those underpaid people in starched uniforms are on our side. In spite of high costs and other evidence to the contrary, hospitals are not out to get us. It's silly to go through life running from things that are not after us. To do so is to transform a fear of hospitals into fear of living.

So, let's celebrate the people and places which improve our health and add years to our lives. Once we're healthy, our task is to live fully, joyfully, and usefully. It means we may even enjoy the company of medical personnel, and laugh and joke with them—preferably when they're off duty.

4

The Corridors of Life

I am a diabetic. If you read the opening chapter of this book, you already know that. I have been a diabetic for over twenty-five years and many people know because I talk about my illness every chance that I get, in outright bids for sympathy and attention. Why have a debilitating disease and not exploit it as much as possible?

My wife, Nancy, is also a diabetic. She has had the disease for over fifty years. I may have caught it from her. Nancy almost never discusses her diabetes in public because, she says, one Nutra-Sweet talker in a family is enough.

Anyhow, diabetics face two on-going dangers. One is that they will overeat or eat the wrong foods (definition: food that tastes good) and produce blood sugar that is too high. Too-high blood sugar complicates life. It causes every small cut or bruise to heal more slowly. It damages the kidneys. It slows reaction time. Eventually, if not controlled, one falls into a coma and dies—which *really* slows your reaction time.

The other danger is to have low blood sugar or an excess of insulin in your system. This causes insulin reactions. They occur when you exercise more than usual or eat too few calories for the amount of insulin you injected. Low blood sugar probably does less overall harm to your body than high blood sugar, but its effects are more immediate and dramatic.

Nancy has had some interesting, nay, mind-boggling insulin reactions in our life together. Persons having insulin reactions often behave as if they were inebriated. The diabetic functions in a semi-conscious way, and one's speech is both slurred and incoherent. In short, one acts as drunk as a skunk, although smelling somewhat better.

Years ago, for example, Nancy felt an insulin reaction coming on. We went to a restaurant to get a "food fix," but the food was slow to arrive. Nancy's conversation gradually lapsed into senselessness, covering topics such as aliens from outer space. When her food arrived, she delighted in flipping whipped cream toward me and other wide-eyed customers. The evening was memorable. We never went to that restaurant again.

Once she attended a convocation at Earlham and had another insulin reaction. A friend led her home where we fed her orange juice laced with honey. After she returned to normal, we went back to the campus to find the rest of her clothes.

Because I'm not so brittle a diabetic as Nancy, I've had fewer insulin reactions. And I've had only one when I was not with someone who could help me through it.

I was spending the night in a hotel in Canton, Ohio, where I'd gone for a speaking engagement. Usually I test my blood before going to bed, but I'd forgotten to bring my testing machine. When the alarm went off early the next morning, I awakened out of a deep sleep feeling both grogginess and the early stages of an insulin reaction.

In my befuddlement I decided to go outside my room and pick up the morning paper. Of course there was no morning paper, and when the door locked behind me, I found myself standing in a hotel corridor wearing only my underwear. Not any underwear, mind you, but red undershorts decorated with large valentines Nancy had given me as a gift.

As consciousness slowly returned, I realized my only course of action was to walk down the hallway, past the restaurant full of patrons, through the hotel lobby to the front desk to get another key. This I did with as much dignity as I could muster, which was minuscule. To be fair, the people I met were friendly and smiled a lot; some even laughed aloud. The desk clerk had to know my name and room number before he could give me a key, and he repeated both loudly in case attendants looking for escaped mental patients were nearby.

Planning ahead is essential for diabetics. Anticipating circumstances becomes necessary for people as they grow older and discover that the old gray mare is not what she used to be. We have to allow ample time for getting from point A to point B.

That's as it should be. Trusting that God is with us does not preclude planning and living carefully. Life in the slow lane is still a good life. Taking care of ourselves is as much a form of stewardship as pledging dollars to a church budget. The body is a temple dedicated to God, and temple maintenance is not an edifice complex. Living within our limitations is to cooperate with God's intentions for us, even though occasionally we wander the corridors of life in our underwear.

5

Out of Control

When we become patients in a hospital, we relinquish control over our lives. I re-learned this lesson in the summer of 1995 when, in order to avoid a severe heat wave, I had major surgery in an air-conditioned hospital. It was my fourth stay in five years, but my memory failed to remind me of one important reality. I forgot the fine print in the admission form which forfeits one's rights to any semblance of modesty, privacy, or human dignity.

For example, one's food is carefully measured so that the patient receives precise amounts of protein, carbohydrates, and fat, but the choices are only two—take it or leave it. While some of the food is edible, how does a hospital know to provide you with a diet you would never choose in a restaurant unless on the verge of starvation? Had George Bush been a patient, every meal would have featured broccoli.

I was also connected to a variety of tubes which were in turn joined to a machine that dripped potent medicine with exotic names into my blood stream. That I continued to have a blood stream was a small miracle because early each morning and late each night, people in white coats extracted large quantities of my blood and took it away. This had been done in all my previous visits to hospitals, but I finally figured out what was done with the extra blood. The nurses said it was sent to the laboratory for tests, but it really was used in secret cultic rituals in the basement.

The most memorable—nay terrible—example of being out of control happened two days after my surgery. I was regularly given morphine for pain control, and it eventually triggered the only hallucination of my sixty-one years (if you don't count my six years as Dean of the Earlham School of Religion.)

I awakened out of a restless sleep not knowing where I was or why. I felt bound by the blankets on my bed, as if I were in a straight jacket. I yelled for help or babbled incoherently, my roommate reported later, in a language possibly understood by Martians because it had to do with green slime. When my eyes were closed, squiggly lines floated before me. A moving collage of grainy photographs, none of which could be identified, moved in and out of my mind.

Having some familiarity with the Bible, I know a little about visions and dreams. Ezekiel saw wheels within wheels, and Isaiah imagined seraphim, tongs, and altars. I would have settled for a beautiful woman riding a horse, or even apple pie with ice cream. Instead, I received nothing. Zero, zilch, nada. In my anguish I cried out, "Newt Gingrich, help me!" Of course no help came, so I knew I was returning to the real world.

I made up the last part, but the rest was true. For a period of time, I was one terrified, out-of-control, recently-operated-upon Quaker. As I eased back into awareness, concerned nurses calmed me and gave me the business cards of two social workers and a psychiatrist.

The memory of being totally helpless will not soon be forgotten. Reflecting upon it, however, provides insight. The hallucination, while bizarre, reminded me that we do not have control over our lives in any ultimate sense. We try. We make plans and dream dreams. We fund retirement accounts and set goals for our lives. Part of the time those goals are reached and some dreams come true. When such happens, we can rejoice and be glad.

Other times, circumstances and the vagaries of life remind us that, plan though we may, we do not control outcomes. I did not plan to acquire Crohn's disease. My doctors said that only ten percent of those who earlier have had their colons removed, as I did, later get Crohn's. I like being among an elite group, but this is not what I had in mind.

My wife, Nancy, has taken excellent care of her diabetes since discovering she had the disease at age ten. Even so, she still had to have her leg amputated in spite of the best medical help available and the prayers of countless supporters.

When we lay our plans and dream our dreams, we don't expect cancer, heart attacks, or automobile accidents. But they happen, and it's then we remember that human beings, no matter how virtuous or how faithful, have little control over life's outcomes. We're not ultimately in charge.

But, lest we forget, neither are we alone. Though we can't figure out why good people suffer or why some die and others live, the Christian faith reminds us that God is with us. God's people couldn't prevent my surgery or save Nancy's leg. Nevertheless, they prayed for us and with us. They walked alongside through the valley.

Being loved is the one necessity, the one gift that hallucinations in the night or harsh realities of the day cannot diminish. Being loved by God and God's people is more important than being in control. Like Job, we discover we can trust even when we can't understand. To paraphrase the apostle Paul, " . . .neither death, nor life, nor angels, nor principalities, nor things present, nor things to come, nor Crohn's disease, nor Nancy's amputation, nor anything else in all creation, will be able to separate us from the love of God in Christ Jesus our Lord."

Part II

Vicarious Living

Vicarious: "Acting on behalf of or representing another. Performed or suffered by one person with results accruing to the benefit or advantage of another; substitutional, enjoyed by one person through his/her sympathetic experience of another person."—*Webster's New Collegiate Dictionary*

At some point in his life, a man begins to understand himself differently. At least this man is doing so as he ventures into his seventh decade. He begins to live vicariously.

As a parent I was conscientious in taking care of my children. I looked out for them. I worried about them. I was the caretaker, the one to whom they turned for advice and counsel. In recent years the roles have begun to reverse just as they did between my father and me.

My dad died of cancer when he was sixty-two. In our family he was the breadwinner, even though my mother was always involved in the family business. He was not an articulate man, having no education beyond the eighth grade. But he helped me in countless ways even after I was grown, married, and a parent myself. I continually turned to him for help, particularly in practical matters. He could fix anything, and he assumed the patriarchal role of providing comfort and direction.

It was near the end of his life that I realized our roles had reversed. My parents had moved near our home two years before, and I realized they were looking to me for help and support. Dad's health was poor, and on one occasion I was helping him bathe because he had become very weak. As I helped him out of the bathtub, his emaciated body was a stark contrast to the strong, muscular man I had idolized as a child. When Dad would discipline me as I was growing up, he sometimes remarked that I had to do what he said until I was big and strong enough to "out wrestle him." On that day as I lifted him out of the tub, I said: "Dad, I think I can out wrestle you now."

So we trade places. The caretaker role gradually shifts, and it is as natural as the seasons.

Relationships change in other ways, too. Nancy and I realize that our adult children are our best friends. We talk politics and religion as equals. We enjoy each other's company. The distinction as to who is "in charge" becomes blurred. Liking, as well as loving, one's children is a special blessing from God.

We also see ourselves in our children, our students, or others in whose lives we've been involved. As we grow older, we recognize that the world's realities have affected us. We've become more cautious, less idealistic, often demonstrating an "I've seen it all before" attitude. Discovering this in our lives is not always comforting because most of the causes we championed in our youth retain their urgency now. We've become more conservative. The needs remain to be met.

Those of us who live long enough to see how our students turned out and how our children have embraced our values—or not—are left in a quandary. May we take credit for the virtues and achievements of those we've taught or to whom we have ministered? If so, do we take the blame when the values and beliefs we intended to pass along clearly were not? When we take the Christian faith seriously, looking back on our lives is a sobering experience. At best we can judge our *intentions* and efforts to be faithful, and seek forgiveness for the places we failed.

Finally, those of us who live past sixty and still have the comfort and support of our spouses recognize that our roles also change as husbands and wives. Our daughters have helped me reduce the amount of sexism I once practiced in our marriage by simply pointing it out in gently humiliating ways. But circumstances have caused the greatest changes. When Nancy had a leg amputated, she became more dependent upon me for daily help than either of us had anticipated. Because she valued her independence, it was a setback for her. Since she had invested her life in child and husband care, to let us do the same for her was a major adjustment.

For her husband and her children, however, it was not a payback. It was, instead, an opportunity to show in tangible ways how much she was cherished. At this writing she has not yet been fitted with a prosthesis, so helping her will become less necessary as her mobility increases. Cherishing her, however, will continue as long as we live.

6

Trading Places

The main task of parents is to help children become independent. Each step in that direction increases the freedom of both parent and child.

Chad, my oldest grandchild, became toilet trained fairly late. It seemed to take forever, and we wondered if it would happen before he graduated from college. Once accomplished, many changes occurred—or didn't occur if referring to diapers. No longer did his parents have to carry a suitcase full of stuff every time Chad accompanied them across town. Nor did his mother any longer have to hoist her son up by one leg and sniff him the way a hunting dog traces a raccoon.

When children put themselves to bed, parents have fresh opportunity to become reacquainted. And their child has taken on a new responsibility. When children clean their own rooms, or at least rake them regularly, they're moving toward maturity.

A driver's license increases freedom, too. Teenagers do not have to be hauled to those several events which, if missed, might ruin their lives. They can drive themselves and ruin their own lives. And parents can use the extra time to work longer hours to pay for higher insurance costs on the family car.

Eventually, most children become adults and marry. Some of them get jobs and support themselves. In fact, the old joke applies:

Freedom for parents comes when the children are gone and the dog has died.

Getting to that point, of course, is not trouble-free. Children growing up tend to claim freedom before they're ready for it. We can't pay cash for maturity. It comes only on the installment plan. Along the way parents continue to give advice, but advice is like a laxative. It's easy to take but hard to predict the outcome.

Even so, independence is eventually claimed by our adult children, and sometimes we don't like it. When Sarah, after graduating from college, chose to live in a run-down apartment in center-city Philadelphia that could have made the cover of *Slum Magazine,* I argued against it on grounds of safety, health, and neighborhood. She countered: "Dad, you taught me to live within my income and make friends with my neighbors." It's hard for a father to relinquish his authority, and it's mean of his daughter to quote his own advice back to him.

Martha and her husband are choosing furniture for their new home. Nancy and I have sent several clippings about rugs and furniture. We even offered, nobly, to give them our table and chairs which Nancy's parents had given us. But they didn't want them, even though you can sit on most of the chairs without their collapsing.

Ruth, our youngest daughter, was offered a job as a newspaper reporter in Terre Haute, only four hours from our front door. Instead, she chose to move to California to work there because it was a better quality newspaper and a more challenging job. Proximity to her parents was less important. Who does she think she is? A grown-up?

Don't misunderstand. Our children are kind to us. They always listen to my advice, knowing that it does no harm to listen and makes me feel better by offering it. Occasionally they take my counsel if it agrees with what they intended to do anyway. And I guess I'm glad they're adults and in charge of their lives, particularly since two of them have children of their own who will one day put them through the same experience. Then will scripture be fulfilled, the one that reads "vengeance is mine, says the Lord."

Their independence we can handle. But lately we've noticed another transition is underway. It's subtle but apparent. It's a changing of power, a transfer of responsibility. It's trading places. I noticed it first when I visited Ruth on a trip to California. She drove her car and once, when she suddenly hit the brakes, threw out her arm to protect me from crashing into the windshield. She insisted I wear sunglasses because "you can't be too careful in the California sun." My return flight home necessitated a very early departure. Ruth set her alarm and came in to waken me! My youngest child, the one who literally had to be pried out of bed when she was a teenager, took responsibility for getting her strong and wise father out of bed. I used to turn on all the lights in her room, sing "Joy Is Like the Rain" so loudly the neighbors complained, and—as a last resort—put our wretched dog in bed to lick her awake. Now the awaker had become the awakee.

Last Christmas Sarah felt she should prepare the dinner in order to spare her mother the trouble.

Brett and my son-in-law Charlie show up to take down the storm windows in the spring and put them up in the fall. For the record, I can still do storm windows and would if I had a better ladder.

And why does Martha call her sister when she doesn't find us at home to answer the phone? Nancy and I are entitled to go some places without telling our adult children.

Having a son-in-law who is a cytotechnologist in our local hospital complicates the issue, too. Why else does Charlie, at the dinner table, talk about the new test for prostate trouble? It's not your usual topic of conversation.

So what's going on here? I'm not old. I'm just more mature than I used to be. I need my space. Please, daughter, I'd rather do it myself. And we will do it ourselves. More slowly, perhaps, but it only takes a little longer to open windows of opportunity. In fact, bless their hearts, our children are doing more worrying than anything else. I feel fine except for occasional surgery to remove a vital organ. Nancy will soon win a Joslin award as a fifty-year diabetic, a tribute to good health and a truly wonderful husband.

So, let them worry. It's good practice, and one of the delights of growing older is to become a burden to our children. The good part is in seeing how they love us. It's nice to know because if we ever do need them, in say, twenty years or so, they'll come. I hope they'll call first, however; we may have gone to the movies. The early show.

"So, Dad, did you hear some inventor at the Mayo Clinic has perfected an abdominal zipper? It's the newest rage in vital organ removal. You might wanta check it out."

7

Friends in the Family

Parents do not always enjoy the company of their children. Those of us with adult children often repress the memory of taking youngsters to a sit-down restaurant with tablecloths and silverware and vowing, afterwards, never to be seen in public with them again.

In fast-food restaurants table manners, or the absence thereof, are not significant since sandwiches are served in paper on cardboard and fed to one's self by hand. No one cares if elbows are on a table or french fries fall to the floor. But in places where we actually sit at a table and are served by polite persons who take our orders, small children rebel. They are in a slow-food restaurant, usually dressed in good (i.e, uncomfortable) clothes, and undoubtedly will spill their milk three minutes after it arrives. Parents practice patience, mop up the spills, and pay the bill in cash in an effort to conceal their name and address.

Long motor trips with young children also cause a repression of memories. Twenty minutes after leaving home on a five hundred-fifty-mile vacation trip, one child asks, "How much farther is it, daddy?" Twenty minutes later the other children experience sibling rivalry,a sociological term that covers yelling, arguing over comic books, and spilling a super-size Slurpy all over the back seat. Enjoying the company of young children on a long trip in a small car is a contradiction in terms.

Nor do children always enjoy the company of parents. My youngest daughter, Ruth, revealed that she would never sit next to me when I wore a certain colorful shirt. I thought is was chic to wear a shirt that had different colored sleeves, back and front. Ruth was afraid her friends would see us together.

Both Sarah and Martha recall, with eyes directed heavenward, the time they went to 4-H camp together. In a spirit of levity, I ran alongside the bus as it was departing, yelling, "They're taking away my babies." Their embarrassment was unfounded, particularly since none of their friends could see them crouched on the floor between the seats.

During his teenage years, our son Brett regarded his parents as a necessary evil. We were a source of money, food, and rides to places we weren't going. The pleasure of our company during his teenage years was equal to that which he held for the dentist.

The good news is that NOW they and we enjoy each other. The fact that we were imperfect parents and they were imperfect children has not prevented us from becoming friends with each other as adults.

Part of it is the mother-daughter THING. Our three grown daughters and their mother delight in shopping together. Forgive the vestiges of my male sexism, but I think that women in general—and the women in my family in particular—bond while shopping. The operative word is "shopping" not "buying." They tirelessly peruse stores, fingering garments and muttering "Isn't that darling!" like a Greek chorus at a style show. In between times they sit, drink tea, and talk. Their shared pleasure is obvious.

While I'm excused from shopping, my grown children and I delight in other experiences of close friendship. Sarah is a church secretary, and she and I love to discuss the stuff of church life. Martha and I like fast-action, cliff-hanger movies. We call them "biters," short for "nail-biters." Ruth is a journalist, and the money we spend on long-distance phone calls about her articles could finance a small South American country. Brett and I bond every time he asks for a loan, and over the years we've grown close.

And, of course, there are the grandchildren who are flawless, although, oddly enough, their parents don't enjoy taking them to restaurants. Our grown children enjoy our company in spite of whatever damage this does to their social acceptance.

Nurturing children requires patience and long-suffering. But when those same children grow up and become your friends, it's like a gift from God. When it happens, it's worth all the time, all the worry, and all the trouble invested. It is to be richly blessed.

8

A Graduation Message from God

When I graduated from Kentland, Indiana, high school in 1952, the president of Ball State spoke at our commencement. He said many good words, and his main point was that we, the graduates, were about to go into the world and the future was in our hands.

Four years later the ambassador to Australia addressed my graduating class at Earlham College. He, too, made several important points, the primary one being that the class of 1956 was about to go into the world and the future would be in our hands.

Three years after that commencement the president of Yale University spoke to those of us getting degrees from Yale. His speech was inspiring, and he gave us courage for going into the world where the future would be in our hands.

At that point I entered the world which turned out to be New Castle, Indiana, where I was pastor of the Friends Meeting. Quickly, I learned two things. One, I wasn't really ready for the world and, two, the world was a lot like the places I'd left in order to enter it.

When young people graduate to "enter the world," they usually carry with them enormous idealism and hope. The future, they think, really is in their hands. When I became pastor at New Castle, I fully expected a large hunk of the Kingdom of God to be ushered in as a result of my hard work and dedication no later than the third Thursday of the fourth month.

Thirty years later it has become obvious that hard work, dedication, and sincerity—or reasonable facsimiles thereof—have not necessarily produced moral reformation, a dramatic increase of faith, and an outbreak of Christian living. We did establish an excellent tradition of first class coffee-hour fellowships in two Meetings, however, and thirty years at Earlham have caused no serious harm.

Nevertheless, as most folks who have been in ministry for thirty or forty years will testify, good intentions and noble efforts do not always produce positive results. In fact, many churches have lost members, and society in general seems less moral and more adrift than ever.

One incident from my own ministry illustrates the point. Over one six-month period when I was a pastor, I immersed myself in a counseling relationship with a couple headed for divorce. I employed all the counseling training I had learned at Yale. I listened carefully and met with them faithfully. Even so, about the only point on which the couple could agree was that I was a meddlesome jerk who should butt out. Blessed are the would-be peacemakers if they don't get clobbered in the process!

Nor has growing older and theoretically wiser been much help in changing the world for the better. Becoming wiser has simply reminded me that everything is more difficult than I once thought. There are always root causes beyond my control, long-range consequences we can't see, and a larger picture that must be taken into account. All we can do is apply an occasional Band-Aid to a problem that will return again and again: "Human nature doesn't change." "There will always be wars and rumors of wars." "The poor will always be with us." Etc., etc., etc.

Instead of telling starry-eyed graduates that they are about to go into the world where the future is in their hands, the temptation is to advocate a ritual cleansing that is at least realistic. Perhaps we should look heavenward, point our diplomas toward the sky, and chant in unison three times, "Oh, ain't it awful!" Then, over refreshments, we can blame everything on Bill Clinton or the Republicans—both of whom are likely candidates for blame. I'd do it too, if it weren't for the cap-and-gowned idealists who näively think they can change the world. My own children, who ought to know better from simply observing their father over the years, still believe in progress. My daughters are passionately committed to peace because they don't want their infant sons one day to kill or be killed in wars that old politicians start. They're like their mother who recycles cans, writes her congressman, prays for Arabs, and sends baby clothes to Lebanon.

Most graduates would refuse to chant, "Oh, ain't it awful!" and instead hop up and down and shout, "What a chance to make a difference!" I know Earlham School of Religion graduates who ignore the seven last words of a Quaker Meeting, i.e., "We never did it that way before." They expect to try something new!

My job as a veteran Quaker is to warn all the idealists before they expend all their energy, ideas, and dedication on Band aids and good deeds. So, listen up graduates....

Editors note: At this point Tom Mullen's ending was cut short and the following message inserted in its place. We asked Tom who had written the message. He nervously glanced upward and said nothing.

"Shutteth up, Mullen. In your whining about 'realism' you've forgotten the main point of the Gospel. I never promised that good works would be rewarded or that good results be the outcome of dedicated service. I only promised to be with you in the effort and that my Grace would be sufficient. Ultimately, My will is going to be done. The future is in My Hands. Idealism and Hope are sources of power, so let them flow like a river. And try to be more like your wife and kids. Amen."

9

Credit or Blame?

I've always enjoyed mowing the grass and working jigsaw puzzles. What do they have in common? I can tell when I'm finished. I can see the results of my efforts.

The results for the rest of my work are not so clear. For all of my adult life, my primary roles have been preacher, teacher, and parent. In these roles we have to wait a long time to see if our efforts have made any difference. In the *middle* of preaching, teaching, and parenting, we can't always tell. And even if we see good outcomes, so many other factors enter in that it's hard to identify cause and effect.

We hope that there is a cumulative positive effect from the work of a pastor. By a loose calculation I've preached well over two thousand sermons. Some of them were good, most were sincere, and a few merely filled a slot in a Sunday service. But what has been remembered? Were lives really touched? Such questions arise when a student, who had heard me preach many times, commented after a worship service: "Tom, every one of your sermons is better than the next!"

Or I recall the elderly man I visited regularly when I was a pastor. He usually said the same things each time I visited, told the same stories, and repeated identical phrases. On one of my visits I fell into the trap of not really listening to his words but, instead, substituting nondirective phrases that counselors often use: "uh huh" "yes" "uh huh." His rambling went on and my robotic muttering became a continual response. At one point he seemed to come awake and asked point blank, "Is uh-huh all you can say to me?" I was still on automatic pilot, so I replied, "uh huh."

Do preaching and pastoral care make a difference? It's hard to know because the answer lies in the hearts and minds of the people we serve.

It should be easier to determine cause and effect with teaching. After all, students are graded along the way, and many of them compliment their teachers when they graduate. If they don't make it through, fewer compliments are forthcoming. One graduate, groping for words, said: "Of all the teachers I've ever had, you've been one of them." Education is what happens between classes. And the disconcerting fact remains that the best students learn however well or poorly we teach, and the most we can take credit for is pointing them in a useful direction.

Furthermore, it's hard to know what your work has accomplished when you recall those students who resisted all your efforts to help them learn. For years I taught an undergraduate course at Earlham College called *Introduction to the Bible*. It was one of those courses that sectarian colleges have in the curriculum for students who want to fulfill a religion requirement as painlessly as possible.

I loved teaching the course because I enjoyed the challenge of introducing the Bible to persons who had either little knowledge of it or else a bias against it. However, one student resisted all my efforts to take the course seriously. I gave him individual tutoring. I substituted a "creative project" for one of the exams. Everything I tried was treated with total lack of interest. Eventually, I exploded and yelled at him, "John (not his real name) I can't tell whether your problem is ignorance or apathy." He replied, "I don't know and I don't care!"

Teachers, by definition, live vicariously through their students. The hard question is: If I take credit for those who go on to do well, must I take blame for those who don't?

Parenting is, in general, more easily analyzed in terms of cause and effect. We know that good parents who are committed to child-rearing and love their children will probably see them grow into responsible, secure adults. Why, *precisely*, children in the same family grow into adulthood with diverse values, religious beliefs, and behavior patterns is not so clear. Many other influences shaped their outcomes.

My youngest daughter is a journalist on a large metropolitan newspaper. I read each of her articles with interest and pride. I half-jokingly tell friends that now my life is over, I live vicariously through her work. I long to take credit for her, but her mother, her peers, her teachers, and—mostly—she herself have a righteous claim on her becoming the excellent human being she is.

Our oldest daughter is a better Quaker-Christian than her parents and a better parent to her son than we were to her. She's secure in who she is, and uses her Phi Beta Kappa intelligence in her roles as mother, spouse, church secretary, and para-legal. I'd love to say, "See what we have produced!" but others have nurtured her, too, and the reason she is a warm, caring person surely is a gift from God.

The middle daughter has always been the life of our family party, full of mischief and fun. She, also, was an excellent student and has two vivacious children just like herself. Her personality attracts friends like bees to honey, and every time she comes to visit, we clear our calendars so that we can celebrate each moment she's here. I want to believe that her love of life is a gift we gave her, but it came from many sources and, ultimately, from God.

My son is very different from his sisters. He resisted education from kindergarten through high school, finally graduating in the upper quarter of the bottom fiftieth of his class. He cares little for church, has values that starkly contrast with his parents, and has interests that cannot be traced, even by Sherlock Holmes, to our family. He has been our clearest reminder that children are not white mice who are run through mazes until they emerge at predictable places.

Living in relationships means living vicariously, and we have no final control over the outcomes of our children, students, or friends. We are responsible for *obedience*, not results. We're called to be the best parent, teacher, preacher, or candlestick maker we can be, and the outcomes are in the hands of God.

To take credit or blame is, after a point, a futile activity. Happiness is experienced when life gives us what we are willing to accept. Rejoicing in what has been given us is not always easy, and all of us look back and find some small or large reason for regret. But Garrison Keillor is correct when he writes: "Some luck lies in not getting what (we) thought (we) wanted but getting what (we) have, which, once (we) have it (we) may be smart enough to see is what (we) would have wanted had (we) known."

Life is a gift, one shared with others that, as we look back, is the best gift we could have received.

10

Cherishing One Another

Couples married a long time anticipate each other's needs. Nay, at times they read each other's minds.

For example, the following conversation took place between Nancy, my wife of almost forty years, and myself:

Nancy: "Tom, what would you like for breakfast?"

Tom: "Let's have pancakes smothered in butter and drenched in sugar-free syrup."

Nancy: "Oh, you don't want that, do you?"

Tom: "No, but for a minute I thought I did."

Happily married people accept each other, idiosyncrasies and all. We learn to enjoy a comfortable familiarity that replaces any tendencies to reform or "fix" one's mate early in a marriage. While both partners change over time, a basic acceptance of each other's peculiarities is essential. Morning people sometimes marry night people, and the marriage survives. Some folks can't function without a morning cup of coffee. Others come alive at sunset.

One woman was asked if she woke up grouchy in the morning. She replied: "No, he sets the alarm and gets up by himself." That's acceptance.

More important than acceptance, however, is what couples sometimes experience as their marriage continues over decades. It is the cherishing of one another.

Cherishing often starts out as a matter of looking after one another or fulfilling a husbandly or wifely role. Most men of my generation, i.e., born in the 1930's, grew up expecting a woman to take care of them. My mother took care of my father and her two sons, and I entered marriage with the assumption that Nancy would take care of me.

When I wanted a clean shirt, I went to my closet and lo, it was there. Should I discover a sock that needed mending, I set it aside and eventually small elves darned it. I asked the question, What's for dinner? because the assumption was that fixing meals was the wife's responsibility.

To be fair to me, I mowed the grass, made the bed, cleaned the basement, and sometimes ran the sweeper. We often eat out in restaurants, too, which frees both of us from several tasks. But fairness also dictates that I *own* the fact that women in my life— a mother, a wife, and sometimes a daughter—have looked after my daily well-being.

How firmly these patterns had been established became clear when Nancy slipped on the ice one winter and broke her right arm. Her arm was placed in a hard cast bent at the elbow, pointing upward with only her fingers exposed. She appeared to be perpetually waving. The several weeks she wore the cast turned out to be, as they say in church, a transforming experience.

Not only did I have to sleep on the opposite side of the bed to avoid being bonked in the middle of the night, many other adjustments had to be made. I learned that elves in fact had not been doing the laundry. Bologna sandwiches are less delicious the fourth night in a row. Out of necessity, I became more of the housekeeper than I had ever been, and my devotional life was enriched as a result. I prayed earnestly for a rapid healing of Nancy's arm.

More enlightening, however, was the fact that I had to take care of her in ways I had not anticipated years before when I promised to be faithful in sickness and health, for better or worse. I had to fold her laundry, wash her back, and help her get dressed. A right-handed person who fractures her right arm becomes suddenly dependent.

I had to take over the family bookkeeping, even though Nancy tried to write checks with her left hand. In spite of her illegible handwriting and my negligence, several of our bills were paid on time and nasty letters from creditors eventually stopped coming.

The task, however, that I never fully mastered was helping her dress. I've long felt that women's clothes have been designed by sadists who assume their clients are either contortionists or double jointed. How else can we explain blouses that button in back, shoes with straps that never fit the heel, and dresses that have to be pulled into place.

Hardest of all was helping Nancy put on pantyhose. I confess I had never paid close attention to the intricacies of getting this garment onto a woman's body. It shouldn't have been difficult; after all, they're just long, thin socks, aren't they? So I put them on her feet and then attempted to pull them up. Wrong. They had to be gradually rolled up the leg, making sure no wrinkles emerge in the process. It also helps to start them on the right feet in the first place. And it doesn't help at all to put them on from behind your wife while she is laughing hysterically and occasionally bonking your head with her cast.

Looking out for one another till death us do part is more than a vow. It is the practice of cherishing one another. It is mature love. Harry Stack Sullivan says that we love a person when the security and well-being of another becomes as significant as our own security and well-being.

Indeed. Blessed are they who discover that doing the laundry, scrubbing the toilets, and fixing meals are ways of cherishing the one you love. Given the hazards of married life and the fear and trembling that long-term commitment causes, romantic passion is an easier sell than mature love. But for those who experience God's providence and share a long-term marriage, cherishing one's mate is worth the investment of time, commitment, and damaged pantyhose.

Part III

The Second Time Around

Those of us with grandchildren get to see Scripture fulfilled, the passage that, paraphrased, says "Raise up a child the way he should go and when you are old you'll wish you'd done better." We re-live certain indelible moments and recall others with a mixture of humor and chagrin.

Remembering is one of God's gifts. And so is learning what your grown children remember from their upbringing. Family histories are partly cyclical. We repeat, sometimes, the very words of advice our parents gave to us, and every so often we hear our counsel passed along by our adult children to their progeny. Thus, we re-remember.

Most families establish certain rituals. For years our nuclear family celebrated Christmas with my side of the family on Christmas Eve. The next day we packed everybody into the car and drove to Indianapolis to do Christmas with Nancy's parents. When the children became college students, we declared that 233 College Avenue was the homeplace and family should come to us. Eventually our widowed mothers started joining us for the holiday.

Re-remembering is selective. I tend to forget that my parents were separated for a year when I was a junior in high school. I happily remember the joyful day my father returned home and my parents reconciled. I recall with a blend of sadness and satisfaction when our children joined us around their grandmother's grave and shared memories of what that fine lady meant to them.

Families have histories, and it's important children discover they are extensions of that history. They'll correct mistakes their parents made, and they'll make new ones of their own. But the umbilical cord of a family is seldom neatly severed. It stretches across years, generations, and the stretching shapes family identity.

We're WASPS, White Anglo-Saxon Protestants. We're products of the Puritan ethic, so we've valued hard work and clean living. We're Quakers, members of the Religious Society of Friends, which means we hold a sectarian view of life and accept the fact that our ways do not always conform to society's. Our children and theirs can accept or reject this family history, but they'll have to deal with it.

The culture of a family sometimes causes problems across generational lines. The temptation for grandparents to interfere in the upbringing of their grandchildren is seductive. Yet times change and nurturing values today is a strikingly different task from doing so twenty-five years ago. Television has to be monitored more closely than ever, and computer networks have allowed more information and more garbage to enter the home.

Thus, staying quiet and keeping our plentiful grandparently wisdom to ourselves, unless asked, is wise. Besides, most of what we have to teach our grown children about parenting has already been learned—or not.

What grandparents can do is celebrate the lives of those little creatures their grown children have provided. Yes, we know that some people our age have no grandchildren, and we're aware they're perfectly happy—and certainly wealthier. Yet, those of us who are grandparents do well to rejoice. My brother, a widower with no children of his own, has embraced his nieces and nephew and their children as his own. This pleases them, and, I think, pleases him as well. And when he's had enough of the uncle role, he simply goes home.

As Tolstoy said, "Happy families are all alike; every unhappy family is unhappy in its own way." Many of you will identify with our family. Remembering and re-living the adventures of a happy family is to be twice blessed. It's an occasion for rejoicing the second time around.

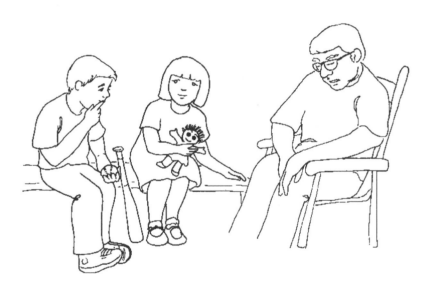

"Sh-h-h. Don't wake him up or we'll have to listen to another one of those stories."

11

The Good Old Days

More and more I sound like my father. My sentences often start with "When I was a boy..." or "I remember the time...." They also frequently end with dramatic illustrations of how hard I worked as a boy, how many miles I walked to school, and how deep the snow was through which I had to walk.

My memory bank is obviously not mathematically precise, and it tends to add one extra mile and one inch of snow for every year over age twenty. Which means that by the time I'm sixty-five, I will remember walking forty-three miles through four feet of snow. In the month of May!

Given the freedom selective memory provides, I also recall delivering newspapers every day after school, cleaning my room each Saturday until it sparkled, and attending Sunday school, worship and youth group with boundless energy and enthusiasm. Indeed, half the fun of nostalgia lies in the editing, and nothing makes the old days good like a poor memory.

Many who long for the good old days are the first to complain when the television goes on the blink. The truth is, today's comforts far surpass yesterday's, and a recent poll revealed that Americans most frequently complain about (1) how to lose weight and (2) where to park the car. Might the two be connected?

I remember getting a postcard from a relative (note: on my wife's side) who complained about her vacation in Hawaii. It seemed a new hotel was being built next to hers on Waikiki beach, and the workers made so much noise she couldn't take naps in the afternoon. Not being able to sleep in the middle of the afternoon in a luxury hotel overlooking a Hawaiian beach is, at worst, a mild adversity.

Let's face it. Life today in terms of physical comforts is softer than it's ever been, at least for the huge middle class of America. Super highways make long trips shorter. Air conditioning makes travel tolerable. And most of us over fifty enjoy ease of living to a degree we could not have imagined in the "good old days." A visit to Conner Prairie Historical Settlement which shows life in Indiana around 1820 reminds us that most Americans worked hard every day just to survive, not to accumulate wealth or build monuments to themselves. An accurate remembering of the past reveals that what was good was that the days were old but we weren't. Nostalgia provides a desire to repossess what we never had.

Better to rejoice in what we do have. An ancient saying puts it succinctly: "My grandfather cleared the land so that his children could raise crops and his grandchildren write poetry." That's not to say that writing poetry or singing songs or painting pictures should be postponed until all our practical needs are met. It is to say that *how* we use the time once spent in *surviving* is a matter of Christian stewardship.

Some choose neither to write poetry, nor sing songs and certainly not to answer a call to serve God in a jungle. Instead, they opt to attempt feats of physical strength or daring that deny age, experience, or common sense. Television commercials show men and women older than I am water skiing without skis or bungy-jumping after drinking Geritol. One television special described a group of citizens, some in their sixties, who had just taken up rock-climbing. Another man in his seventies reported in glowing terms the thrill of shooting rapids for the first time.

Perhaps it's jealousy or cowardice, but if I happen to live in an era when I no longer have to spend all my time and energy either clearing the land or farming the farm, risking my life to prove I'm still able has little appeal. Don't misunderstand. I'm willing to take physical risks, such as crossing the street or teaching graduate students. And I've been known to step boldly onto an escalator without grabbing the handrail! Regularly, too, I walk briskly to Hardee's for breakfast, ready to do battle with cholesterol and calories.

Nevertheless, one of my hopes upon graduating from middle age is that I would no longer have to prove my physical dexterity or prowess. By now, most of my vital juices are prune. I got sick to my stomach when, years ago, I rode with my children on the ferris wheel. Why ride it with my grandchildren when I didn't enjoy it the first time?

Still, we are called to do the moral equivalent of writing poetry and singing songs. Unless we've died—and we'd know that by reading the obituaries—we've been given time to do more than merely survive. We have gifts to give and time to share.

Living in the past has only one advantage. It's cheaper. But rejoicing in the past by passing along our stories to younger generations is a blessing. When my grandmother was a young woman, she worked as a cook during round-up time on the prairie. She would accompany the chuck wagon out to feed the cowboys who were herding cattle. What stories she had for her grandchildren. My father owned a grocery store and service station in Montmorenci, Indiana, and his stories from the days of my infancy were fabulous—and some of them were true. I delighted in his account of the times he waited on the infamous John Dillinger. And the time twenty-three snowbound travelers spent five days in our store and home, captive to the storm. All of them, Dad said, eventually paid him every penny they owed, and I learned early what honesty looked like. And he told about.... Well, you get the idea.

Churches and families need old-timers to pass along their histories to more recent arrivals, some of whom are tempted to think nothing old is worth remembering. True, some memories deserve to be forgotten and some traditions outlive their usefulness. But many provide historical memory that is essential to a family's or a congregation's identity.

Old-timers have to offer more, however, than a connection to the past. They also can burst forth with a new passion or a fresh enthusiasm that startles all around them, particularly their spouses. Such people never retire. They simply stop working at one job in order to do another. They may join the Peace Corps or enter seminary in response to a call from God.

I know one couple who, in their late fifties, adopted five elementary-age children and nurtured them to adulthood. They loved children and were convinced that having a second family was, for them, a source of joy and purpose in their lives together. I admire them, but for me to do that would be like cleaning the oven every day. Yet the spirit of what they did makes the point that to be alive is to live with purpose and enthusiasm. It is sometimes referred to as doing the Will of God.

So let's tell our stories and live our lives, whatever our age. The worst harm we can do is to bore people instead of letting television bore them for us. The best gift we can give is to share our humanity, our hopes, and our enthusiasm. And the world needs all three. Desperately.

12

Re-remembering

When I asked my children what they most remembered from their growing up years, I was surprised by their responses. I expected them to recall SIGNIFICANT EVENTS (e.g., joining the National Honor Society) or LIFE CHANGING OCCASIONS (e.g., going to the Junior Prom).

Not so. Mostly what they remembered were isolated incidents that somehow stuck in their memory banks. Furthermore, the incidents they recalled with pleasure, I remember as mixed with a heavy dose of pain.

Our youngest daughter, Ruth, recalled one particular snow-filled day when she was seven. We were hit that year with a mini-blizzard, and I had returned home from a trip to be greeted by Ruth's passionate plea to take her sledding. Since I had been gone for four days giving speeches telling families to spend more time together, the moral imperative was clear.

An adult perspective on snow is radically different from a child's. Children love snow. The more there is of it, the better they like it. In fact, the joy felt at the sight of freshly fallen snow is inversely proportional to the age of the beholder.

It's different for adults. While it is theoretically true that nothing in nature is more beautiful than a single snowflake, seldom do they come that way. From a grownup's perspective the best thing that can be said of snow is that it makes your own lawn look as nice as your neighbors. As one deservedly unknown philosopher said, "More people would be satisfied with their walk in life if they didn't have to shovel it."

As Ruth remembered it, going sledding that day was a happy time from beginning to end. In my memory, the end was far better than the beginning or the middle.

Getting a seven-year-old dressed for zero weather is a valid study of thermodynamics and motion. By the time Ruth was dressed in long underwear, heavy pants, two pairs of socks, a sweater, a heavy outer coat, a six-foot scarf, cap, ear muffs, and gloves, she moved with all the grace of a penguin. And, of course, as I tied the final knot in her scarf, she urgently needed to go to the bathroom. Now I know why Eskimo families are quite small.

Eventually we made it to the sledding site which is the cemetery adjacent to the college campus. It is an excellent location, as the hills are just right for sledding and navigating among the gravestones provided a special challenge. Ruth enjoyed the experience more than I did as she rode the sled down and her pack-animal father pulled her back to the top.

Late in the afternoon we played a game called pancake. A large person (e.g., father) was spread-eagled on the sled with numerous small children stacked on top of him. The most memorable ride of the day was highlighted by our sled-load of bodies being propelled over the hill at the very moment one of the children pulled the father's stocking cap over his glasses, thereby obstructing his vision so that he could not see the various obstacles in the way of progress.

One by one the bodies of small children rolled off my back until no one of any importance remained. I managed to bail out before the sled made a direct hit on somebody's final resting place but not before I slid another ten feet into Clear Creek, the ice-encrusted stream at the foot of the hill.

Ruth and her friends greatly enjoyed my up-to-the-elbows plunge into the creek, as the sight of a grown man's posterior protruding from a freezing stream inspired a chorus of squeals and laughter. At least the plunge forced a conclusion of sledding for the day, and I had taken one small step for fatherhood and one bone-crushing plop for Blue Cross. Later, minus two tons of coats and sweaters, we nestled in front of a crackling fire, sipping sugar-free hot chocolate between the rhythmic sniffing of runny noses. Both Ruth and I remember this part the same way, even though it happened over twenty years ago.

We remember the good feeling that comes from blood circulating through your body bringing warmth and sensation back to toes you thought were lost forever. We recall the closeness, the intimacy we felt when Ruth snuggled on my lap. The hot chocolate we drank was the best ever prepared, and no Hollywood entertainment could match our silent joy while watching the fire.

Memories are like sledding. They include both ups and downs, but it is a mark of enormous satisfaction to hear one's grown children say, "We had a happy childhood."

The down side of memories can fade away, even the frostbite. What's left is the awareness that we've been blessed by God.

13

Grandchildren and the Meaning of Life

We have three grandchildren. Chad lives only three miles away. The other two, Taro and Hanako, live in New York which is farther. All play a major role in our lives wherever their geographical location. The well-being of our grandchildren is never far from our thoughts or our pocketbooks.

The perspective of grandparents is influenced by the fact that they are interested, but not ultimately responsible, parties in the upbringing of grandchildren. Right now we are in the early stages of grandparenting. The children, ages six, four, and two, need us to baby-sit, but they re not old enough to borrow the car. Their energy is boundless, and they are unpredictable. We never know how high up the wall they're about to drive us. It's true that grandchildren are a comfort in our old age, but our three are helping us reach it a lot sooner. The only things children wear out faster than shoes are grandparents.

Thus, the first difference between parenting and grandparenting is that it takes longer to rest than it does to get tired. We try to compensate by wisdom and careful planning. In our house we've rearranged our possessions so that everything breakable is up high. We know never to awaken a sleeping grandchild just to see her smile.

Chad's parents restrict his watching of television. Videos, we feel, don't count, so we provide wholesome, uplifting, character-building video tapes that he will watch while we catch our breath. He sees them often because we run out of breath quickly. Storytelling is one of the best ways to entertain a four-year-old. It is important that the selective memory of a grandparent be given free rein so that a grandchild can learn how absolutely interesting the life of his courageous, kind, creative, wonderful grandfather has been. Hence, telling one's own story to children should never be done in front of ear witnesses. Since telling stories to children is almost always done sitting down, embellishing history seems a small moral compromise to make in order to avoid considerable physical deterioration.

Small children are innocent enough to believe our stories. When our own children were small, I took them to the place where I was born. The house in which I was born was torn down years ago to make room for a four-lane highway. Directly over the spot where I entered the world now hangs a flashing yellow light that marks an intersection. I told my children—and they bought it—that the highway department had put that flasher there in honor of my birth place. Of course, for several years I was asked, "Who was born there?" every time we saw a caution light!

Nancy and I admit our prejudices toward Chad, Taro, and Hanako. After all, nothing makes a boy or girl smarter than being a grandchild. We are faster on the draw than the Lone Ranger when we reach for pictures of the kids. We interrupt conversations to report Hanako's latest two-year-old achievements, such as throwing a ball or saying "da" in Japanese. We regard Chad's tendency to smear his vegetables in peanut butter as creative nutrition. His recent scientific experiment of borrowing an egg from the refrigerator and using the heating duct as an incubator demonstrated near-genius, we thought. And learning how to remove egg yolk from a metallic grill was educational for his mother as well.

Chad is creative. He can operate a VCR, the dishwasher, and almost any simple mechanical toy. Another simple thing he operates is his grandfather. On occasion, when I attempt to put him to bed, I discover negotiating skills and delay tactics that would make Henry Kissinger proud. He manages to turn bath time into a prolonged adventure. Certainly he needs to take baths, and someday science may be able to explain why a six-year-old cannot walk around a mud puddle. And nothing makes a child more affectionate than sticky hands. All a child ever needs to do to lose weight is take a bath.

Chad's tub is full of floating toys, the peculiarities of which must be carefully demonstrated to the grandparent (sucker) several times. His parents know the routine. The grandparents are less familiar so the one hour bath becomes commonplace. After his bath I put him to bed—for the first time. Then comes the reading of books, the pages of which, if skipped, will cause psychological damage. Two drinks of water and the search for a favorite stuffed animal later, he's back in bed. After a while, when we hear the patter of footsteps, we hope it's a burglar.

We know what he's doing but we don't care very much. Yes, parents have to discipline their children, for if they don't a child will grow up and sow enough wild oats to make a grain deal with Russia. But nothing is harder than having to watch a grandchild being disciplined—even when he needs it. Grandparents *must* worry about their grandchildren—it's our job. If Nancy gets cold in the middle of the night in Richmond, she wonders if Hanako in New York is covered. We may worry more than we did when our own children were small. Then we had only Dr. Spock. Our grandchildren's parents have a book for every problem. Thus, Chad, Taro, and Hanako get spoiled because their parents feel awkward about disciplining Nancy and me.

So, we try to interfere as little as our hearts and minds will allow. Because their parents want the children to eat properly, we refrain from giving them Easter bunnies made of chocolate and nestled in green cellophane grass. Instead, we buy molded yogurt

So, we try to interfere as little as our hearts and minds will allow. Because their parents want the children to eat properly, we refrain from giving them Easter bunnies made of chocolate and nestled in green cellophane grass. Instead, we buy molded yogurt bunnies wrapped in seaweed. We don't buy them everything they want because the surest way to make it hard for children is always to make it soft for them. Nevertheless, it's not easy because we have so many hopes for them that keeping a proper distance between our sentiment and their best interests is difficult. Thus, when we send small packages to Taro and Hanako, we're careful not to cry as tears smudge the address. And it doesn't help their parents to know how much we long to see them.

The peculiar relationship between grandparents and grandchildren is a metaphor for Christian living. Effective Christian loving is finding ways of expression that have the long-range best interest of others at heart.

However useful the relationship between grandparents and grandchildren is as a metaphor, a complete generalization cannot be made. For when that little child grabs your leg right before he goes to bed and says, "G-nite, granddan, I love you lots," all generalizations are off. Such moments transcend analogies. They are signs of the Real Presence of God's love in the world.

"Wow, I got jelly beans and Chocolate eggs in <u>my</u> basket!
What did you get, Chad?"

14

Backward Looking

The temptation to re-play our parenting experience is selective. Inevitably we compare our own upbringing to that which we provided our children and, eventually, to the way our grandchildren are being raised. It's a futile exercise for two reasons: (1) the times have changed and (2) our memories have become blurred.

I remember myself as a dutiful child, obedient to my parents, and cooperative with other children. I remember my children as being *mostly* that way, except for lapses caused by chromosomes from their mother's side of the family. I observe my grandchildren's upbringing and wonder: Is it harder now to bring up children in the way they should go?

For one thing, it costs more. Parents do not bring up children these days; they finance them. Whatever the deduction IRS allows for children, it is not enough. Those who determined the amount of tax exemption for children were either raised by werewolves or their kids teeth came in straight. A recent federal study estimates that it costs sixty-thousand dollars to raise a child from birth through high school, not counting what grandparents kick in for Easter clothes.

Where does it all go? Contrary to parental estimates, most of the money does not go for pizza and soft drinks. Less than ten thousand dollars per year is spent on such items, and much of that amount goes to feed friends of your grandchildren who seldom eat at their own homes.

Children's eating habits cannot be blamed for all the costs, however, as many expenses would happily be forgone had children a choice. Well-balanced meals, haircuts, and piano lessons fall into this category. Having been denied certain cultural advantages ourselves, our generation paid for trips to museums and sets of encyclopedias for our children. They are doing the same for their progeny. Most children, however, prefer being denied those privileges themselves.

Medical care for children costs more today. Obstetricians give way to pediatricians who are supplanted by family physicians who share medical dollars with dentists, orthodontists, and dermatologists. Preventative medicine is almost as expensive as having illnesses, but the number of broken arms, allergies, and pimples children have increases the cost of raising children. The cost also varies in relation to the doctor's rent district and the number of times a physician's office is refurbished. If most serious childhood diseases have been eradicated, why does it cost so much to keep my grandchildren healthy?

The lives of our grandchildren are also much more organized than either our children's or our own were. When I was a boy (I love that phrase!) we played basketball and baseball every chance we got. Now young boys and girls play in leagues. They wear matching uniforms. They don't play, they compete.

Grandparents are part of the problem. When they attend games in which a grandchild is performing, they become emotionally involved. When a young child signs up to play peewee baseball or flag football, spectatorship and participation blend in a unique way. When one's grandson gets a hit, *mild* involvement disappears faster than a ten-run lead in a little league game.

Parents and grandparents pace the sidelines, leap for rebounds, and yell a lot. This over exuberance leads to exaggeration, such as urging an eight-year-old who still sleeps with a night light to "go out and smash them." A few spectators may even direct officials to warmer destinations or reveal interest in their family tree. Wisdom doesn't always come with age. Sometimes age shows up all by itself. The question is: Can our grandchildren have fun or do they always have to compete?

And what about behavior? My own father was the Head of the House. As a result decisions were seldom arrived at by democratic process. I loved him, feared him, and decided early to do parenting differently with my own children. So we negotiated lots of issues, but our children turned out well anyway. My parents didn't always agree with the way we brought up our four children, but they didn't interfere.

And now we silently raise our own questions. Why don't they put children to bed earlier at night? ("Because their father gets home late from work, and he likes to share that task. Fathers do that now, you know, Dad.") Should my grandson get away with insisting that he wear a sheriff's badge to church every Sunday? Or a firefighter's hat? ("Dad, he loves going to Sunday School, and we choose not to hassle him about his outfit. Chad thinks church is the place God goes to have fun.")

My grandchildren are allowed to snack more than is good for them, we think, and they force me to share my goodies with them. Children are natural mimics, too. They act like their parents—and their grandparents—in spite of every effort to teach them good manners.

The temptation of grandparents is to look for outcomes before the process is completed. Children start bringing up their parents about two years earlier than our children started changing us. And when I think back to my own childhood, it's obvious I was well past puberty before I knew what it was.

Grandparents have the constitutional right to make private judgments and a moral obligation to keep quiet. My daughters who have children of their own are going through the same dilemmas we went through with them. Only there are more choices to be made, more pressures to feel, more opportunities to manage.

That's why the Christian faith is a necessity for good parents and a useful resource for grandparents. God was with us when we struggled to nurture our children, and God is a present help now. Our children are better parents in many ways than we were, and we corrected some mistakes our parents made with us. It helps to remember that, and remembering frees us from fault-finding and allows us to do what good parents are called to do—delight in the gifts from God they've been given.

15

Great Expectations

When Christmas music bombards our ears and television commercials feature Santa Claus, we know Halloween is not far away. Indeed, our expectations for Christmas are raised early and often, and woe to those who long to simplify the season.

Pressure on families to get together sometime around Christmas is enormous. Families travel long distances in bad weather at considerable expense to visit relatives they might fail to recognize on the street. True, some families are *both* related to *and* genuinely fond of one another. But living up to all the expectations Christmas generates is hard to do. And some family gatherings can be a fete worse than death.

Once, many years ago, Nancy's extended family plus my mother and brother gathered in the same house on the same day to celebrate Christmas. Three generations were present, including twelve children (the oldest of whom was thirteen), eleven adults, and a partridge in a pear tree.

The gathering was religiously diverse: Quakers, Presbyterians, Lutherans (Missouri Synod), Disciples, a Jehovah's Witness, and one evangelical pagan. Both political parties were represented, even though one family member privately held that to be a Democrat and a Christian was a contradiction in terms.

Because our extended family is both religiously and politically diverse, we planned our time together with great care. Generational needs were anticipated by both menu and schedule. All the nuclear families pitched in. After the meal we settled into the living room to celebrate Christmas the way God intended it to be celebrated—with joy, dignity, and no yelling.

We planned to read *Luke's* account of the birth story, sing two carols around the piano, and then—in a spirit of love and generosity—open gifts one by one so all could enjoy the moment. Our eyes misted over in joyful anticipation.

However, during the reading of *Luke*, about the moment the angel announces, "Behold, I bring you good news of a great joy...," one of the children (I think it was one of my wife's) accused her cousin of opening a package that did not belong to him, a package that was, in fact, hers. Her remark and his response added little to the intended theme of "peace on earth and good will to cousins."

Their tug-of-war, in fact, triggered an outpouring of package-grabbing, paper-ripping, and parent-child confronting that made a buffalo stampede seem orderly. One cousin managed to poke himself in the eye with a branch from the Christmas tree. Another child took a bite out of an ornament. The only obvious connection to a biblical celebration was that "weeping and gnashing of teeth" occurred. A parent tried to salvage the event by yelling over the chaos, "Remember all these gifts come from Jesus," to which her brother responded, "Then let's send the bill to him."

It was not a high and holy moment in the history of our families, but neither has it ever been forgotten. Over twenty years have passed since that gathering, and no other attempts to gather the entire clan to celebrate Christmas have been made.

Looking back it was clear that by filling a room with gifts for small children, we had built expectations too great for them to handle. We'd been victimized by the commercialism of Christmas. It proved to be insatiable. Commercialism has no limits and is no respecter of good intentions. I once wrote an article criticizing Christmas commercialism and sold it for a handsome fee. So there's good money in anti-commercialism—but extravagant gift buying, wrapping, and displaying build the wrong kind of expectations. In an atmosphere of *wanting*, it's hard to celebrate *giving*.

We also learned that one Christmas expectation—getting along and being nice—is no easier in December than it is in April or October. When my brother and I were growing up, we would sometimes fuss with one another over toys or gifts. Our mother would implore us to behave by saying, "Let's not fight. It's Christmas."

That is a huge expectation to place on the Christmas season. We don't, for example, say "It's Ground Hog's Day. Let's be nice" or "It's George Washington's birthday. Let's not fight!" Yet we expect good behavior at Christmas even though the season breeds anger and jealousy. The Spirit of Christ is a reconciling spirit, but the *way* we celebrate the holiday often works against harmony and goodwill.

Our attempt to do Christmas properly—by reading the Bible and singing carols— never had a chance in the face of a roomful of gifts. If worship—the Christ-mass—is not central, it becomes a sideshow. What happens when Christmas falls on a Sunday? Is attendance at worship up or down? Will opening gifts on Christmas morning take precedence over a worshipful celebration of Jesus birth?

Our extended family had good intentions and, after the chaos had diminished, we enjoyed each other a lot. In the quiet aftermath, our warm feelings for one another were nurtured by Christ's spirit. And our great expectations were not all bad. They show a *belief* in the miracle of Christ's reconciling spirit. We're not condemned to self-centered, grim-lipped indulgence. The Lord, indeed, can come, even though twelve children in a room crowded with presents make it harder for him to enter. Maybe that's why the first Christmas was celebrated in a stable.

Part IV

Spiritual Maturity

If we manage to live past sixty, we ought to be more spiritually mature than when we were younger. If we are just as prejudiced, just as unforgiving, just as hard-boiled as we were when we were twenty, what have we been doing and thinking the last forty years? How has all that Bible reading, Sunday School attending, church going, and prayer saying helped?

Among most church groups, the men and women who carry the primary responsibility for spiritual leadership are called "elders." Sometimes, all this means is that those people have hung around long enough to be granted church seniority. It's better when growing older has been accompanied by spiritual maturity.

The irony is that spiritual maturity is usually most present when the "elders" have regular contact with children and/or the young in heart. Visit a congregation with lots of children and young people, and a quality of vitality and enthusiasm will be present, as well as stuff scattered about and several sights and sounds of modest chaos. Jesus said that unless we become like children, we'll not make it into the kingdom. It's a paradox: Spiritual maturity means child-likeness.

More specifically, a mature Christian continues to be open to God's call. Being "set in our ways" is the special temptation of folks my age. While there are many persons, like Mother Teresa, who minister well past retirement age and seem blessed with the necessary courage to perform new duties that new occasions demand, they are atypical. If spiritual maturity, however, means we're *better able* to hear God's call, then age is not a deterrent to our embracing what God requests.

Just "fitting in" with contemporary society is also a test of spiritual maturity. In the seminary where I work, my fear of technology is well known. I'm happy to have a secretary who uses computers, fax machines, and E-mail to expedite our work. But someone has to call attention to the de-humanizing possibilities of a technological age. Some of my complaints are tongue-in-cheek, but in a variety of ways the old days were better—particularly in our having to deal with others face to face, human being to human being, personality to personality. Even when we appear to be old coots, a message that calls people back to person-to-person relationships is valid.

More difficult to justify is an attitude toward culture which is remarkably different from our growing-up years. When I watch old movies on TV, much of what I see is innocent and morally pure. I remember when married couples in the movies always were pictured as sleeping in twin beds. TV sitcoms featured families that were like the Waltons or the Brady Bunch. It was as if life were shown as we hoped it might be rather than how it really was.

Has the portrayal moved too far? Knowing that shock or the bizarre attracts more viewers (or readers) than the safe or the peaceful does, am I put off just because I'm out of touch or out of tune? Or does a life longer than sixty years provide validation for comparison? Spiritual maturity means to keep an open mind, but J.B. Phillips indicts society when he writes that the "blasé" do not find happiness even though they never worry over their sins. To be trapped by one's age can happen whether we're young or old. And asking legitimate questions of music, movies, and literature is the right, nay the obligation, of folks who were around when old movies, old music, and old books were new.

Spiritual maturity is best measured by our ability to ask the right questions and also act on our values and beliefs. To do less is the mark of doddering old people who become rocking chair quarterbacks when the game is nearly over.

16

Antidotes to Aging

Aging has its own set of temptations. One is the feeling that we've seen it all before and there really is nothing new under the sun. A high percentage of our sentences begin with "When I was a young _____(Fill in the blank with "pastor, teacher, homemaker, farmer, etc.") we did this in that way and that in this way. Our nostalgia gives us away. We discover we're in our dotage—or at least our anecdotage.

Another temptation is to become cynical. Age does not necessarily cause cynicism, and most cynics are persons who found out when they were ten that there wasn't a Santa Claus and are still upset. But reasons for becoming cynical abound, and those who are past middle age tend to believe that politicians are more dishonest than ever, doctors no longer care for their patients, and the milk of human kindness has soured. Scrooge, after all, was an old coot, and "bah humbug" rolls easily off old tongues.

Skepticism, at least, is in order in today's world. Television continually urges us to spend money we don't have to buy things we don't need in order to impress people we don't like. The primary struggle of daily life is to see whether business or government will rip us off first.

So we've learned to clutch our billfolds and purses when a bureaucrat, television evangelist, politician, or banker asks for our trust.

If someone gives an inch, experience teaches us to measure it. Cynics, at their worst, believe there are only two kinds of people we can trust—the dead and the unborn.

A third temptation of aging is to wallow in regrets. Those who succumb to this temptation assume that time has passed us by, and they may even regret sins they had no opportunity to commit. As the proverbial sailor put it, "I wish I had visited Las Vegas *before* I was converted!" The road not taken is greener on the other side of the fence, to mix a metaphor. But wallowing in regrets is like letting your ice cream melt while wishing for apple pie.

None of us would consciously choose to live in the past or become cynical or wallow in regrets. Growing older does not dictate that we yield to geriatric temptations. So how do we resist biting forbidden fruits when we're old enough to know better and our teeth hurt?

Old age is like everything else. To make a success of it, we've got to start young. And think young, too. Thus, the best antidote to the hardening of our spiritual arteries is to be with, around, and near children. Jesus was proclaiming a timeless truth when he told us that "unless we become like children, we shall not enter the kingdom."

Child-like Christians possess an irrepressible youthfulness of heart. Some of them may have creaky bones and white hair, if they have any at all. But child-like Christians still look at the world and the people in it with interest and delight. Children live in the present. To a child at a zoo or on a picnic, there is no tomorrow or any yesterday. A three-year-old responds to people as they are without reference to race, creed, or color. We never need to teach a child when to laugh, only when not to laugh. Children see what is funny, what is interesting, and what is important in life. They haven't had time to have seen it all or become cynical or fill a reservoir with regrets. Children and child-like Christians live in a world where delight is still possible.

When my grandson, Chad, was three, he thought he was a fireman. He wore a red, plastic fire captain's hat everywhere, including Meeting for Worship. After visiting a local firehouse, he slid down imaginary poles and put out make-believe fires with the garden hose. After his parents took him to Disney World where a personal relationship with Mickey Mouse was begun, Chad regarded that comic book rodent as a primary source of authority, e.g., "Chad, Mickey wants you to eat all your green beans!"

Chad and I read books together. Often it is the same book that is read three, four, or five times in one sitting. Woe to the grandfather, also, if pages are skipped or a favorite dinosaur's name is mispronounced.

Our other grandson, Taro, smiles at all creatures great and small. He assumes the whole world is friendly, even adults. Taro thinks his grandfather can sing well, but then he also likes strained peas.

Hanako sometimes lets me hold her, if no other options are available. She possesses a smile that is better than sunshine on a dismal day. She represents hope in a cynical world.

In short, the temptations of age that squelch our spirits are resisted best by trusting, enjoying and delighting in the people and events of life. The way children do. Those congregations that have few small children are at a spiritual disadvantage, even though their worship services will be orderly and marbles will seldom be released from tiny hands to roll noisily down the floor incline during the silence. We're closer to the kingdom when we embrace the world view of young children.

So, thank God for young people, whatever their age. Jesus was right. If we would enter the kingdom, we must grow into childhood, liver spots and all.

17

The Entitlements
of Age

Growing old is a bad news, good news process. The bad news is obvious. Our bodies deteriorate, our careers wind down, and our mail brings at least one advertisement per week for retirement homes.

The good news is that certain entitlements come with growing old. Not only can we get discounts at motels and restaurants, we are treated with deference by younger people. Behavior and attitudes they would criticize when we were younger are tolerated with patience and kindness, the way old dogs are allowed to bark when the wind rattles the door. I'm just past middle age, and already I'm regarded as a "character," not quite eccentric but drawing close.

My children, for example, have finally given up trying to get me to dress better. Having lived through three revivals of the wide necktie and one brief (Thank God!) generation of bellbottom trousers, I am no longer urged to conform to dress codes forced on us by anonymous designers in New York who despise men. Because of surgery I have to wear suspenders rather than belts to keep my pants up. Suspenders, by coincidence, are in style, and young, sexy men wear them as symbolic of active libidos and with-it awareness. I explain why I wear suspenders so as not to betray my age group.

My wife keeps giving away my comfortable clothes just because the pants are shiny or shirts frayed on the cuffs. I had to go to a rummage sale and repurchase my favorite sweater, suffering the indignity of paying only 50 cents for a garment that was just right for my body. Nancy delays mending my pants pockets and seams, hoping I will forget them so she can cut old trousers into pieces and use them for polishing the car. No matter. I'm on to her sinister ways, and my favorite pair of pants this spring celebrates the eleventh consecutive year of covering my rump.

I resist using a computer, a stubborn attitude described in an earlier book. Expensive entertainment offers no appeal. Eating a good meal with interesting conversation is my favorite recreation. And I can sit with eager young Quakers, who want the Kingdom to come by Thursday, and not volunteer. And they seem to understand.

That's a change of attitude. When I was a young pastor, I encouraged a wide variety of experimental worship forms. We made music with guitars instead of pianos. We tried "rap" sessions in place of sermons. One time we tried modern dance in which worship leaders leapt high for the Lord. Variety was the operative word and once when defective wiring caused two overhead lights to sputter, the congregation thought it was another experiment in worship.

Our worship innovations were, indeed, moving as people often got up and left in the middle. Certainly they were satisfying, too, as some said they were never coming back. As a young pastor, however, I felt that experimentation was the right thing to do, and sometimes it was.

Now I enjoy traditional Quaker worship and good sermons with an introduction, three points, and a poem. Three hymns with familiar tunes are just right. And silence, blessed silence, that once prompted twenty glances per minute at my watch, I now regard as a message from God to the world, saying, "Calm down." I am becoming, as they say, "set in my ways."

Persons beyond middle age also find their tastes in entertainment differ dramatically from many contemporary presentations, even those well-reviewed by learned critics. It's as if our age entitles us to an opinion whether or not it is congruent with contemporary taste. Sophisticated critics panned *The Sound of Music*. I have watched it eight times. I recall when songs had words and music, rather than guttural sounds usually associated with dogs in heat. I mourn the passing of the *Bill Cosby Show* and attribute its departure to a CIA plot, or the final evidence of America's moral depravity.

Most of these courageous opinions I keep to myself, as I've learned to be careful about forcing my idiosyncrasies on others. Rather than speaking from experience, from experience, I don't speak.

Besides, while I enjoy the entitlements that come with growing older, they carry sobering questions. True, some of my idiosyncrasies do no harm. It makes little difference to God or human society if my dress is out of style. In fact, one day style will come back and agree with me. Even a watch that doesn't run is correct twice a day.

More troubling for people my age is this: Am I so set in my ways that new truth is ignored? Looking back at youthful impulsiveness reminds us of what fools we used to be, but it can't predict what fools we re going to be. If I'm comfortable in my worship, am I too sleepy to hear God's latest call?

The special temptations for Christians my age are these: 1) Complaining. "We never did it that way before." 2) Complacency. "When I was their age, I was younger." 3) Comfort. "Here am I, Lord. Send someone else."

Fortunately, there are many old people who are young of heart. They show what vibrant, relevant faith looks like, and these folks take away our excuses for lethargic Christianity. Yes, the Mature Years (a euphemism for being too young for social security, and too old to get a better job) give us permission to be characters, dress out of style, and hold strong opinions. They do not, however, justify Pharisaism, hard heartedness, and deafness to the call of God.

God is undoubtedly neutral about most of our idiosyncrasies and cares little about our taste in clothes, music, or forms of worship. We're entitled to be "characters" and out of step with society. But in the middle of growing older comes an ancient call: "Follow me." That means NOW. Idiosyncrasies and all. Without excuses. Amen.

18

Out of Touch, Out of Tune

Concerned about the sex and violence that permeated most American movies, we stopped going to theaters and, instead, subscribed to HBO. This effectively brought sex and violence into the home.

HBO was like a new toy when we initially subscribed. The first film our family viewed together was called *The Rose*. It was based on the life of Janis Joplin, whoever she was, and I had heard the theme song from the movie on the radio. It was a haunting melody, easy on the ears. Thus, the whole family gathered to watch, including my elderly mother whose taste in entertainment extended to but not beyond the *Lawrence Welk Show*.

In an early scene of that movie, the actress who played the Janis Joplin-like character appears on stage in front of a wild and raucous audience. Her opening lines are a series of obscene and sexually explicit phrases to which the movie audience responded enthusiastically.

The audience in my home responded differently. Mother wondered if my subscribing to HBO indicated parental failure on her part. My youngest child, Ruth, was in her early teens, and her main surprise was that I was shocked. Worst of all, my son loved the movie and couldn't wait to see it the next time it was on HBO.

That incident is now several years old. Our subscription to HBO has long since expired, and I am no longer surprised when explicit language or sexual scenes appear in movies. I will even admit that *sometimes* movies carry more power and expose evil as evil *because* of language and scenes that never would have appeared in movies in the 1940's and 1950's. Nonetheless, one obvious characteristic of people my age is the feeling that we're out of touch and out of tune with much of contemporary culture.

Once upon a time, movies were rated on how good they were rather than on who was allowed to see them. Some of today's films have so much violence, they should be shown in black and blue. When a sexy scene is shown, my wife leans over and breathes on my glasses. In some films, this requires a lot of heavy breathing. Other movies are more to be pitied than censored. They have plots that are nonexistent and appeal to audiences with IQ's slightly higher than sea gulls. Fortunately, movies are seldom as wicked and vulgar as the advertisements for them suggest, but this fact is also a commentary on the low esteem in which American audiences are held by Hollywood producers.

To be extraordinarily fair, watchers of old movies will agree that Hollywood has always made films for a simple-minded audience—and many of us qualify. My colleagues and I during coffee breaks often discuss recent movies. I find that the movies I like best let me laugh and feel good about the world when the show is over. My favorite film is *The Russians Are Coming, The Russians Are Coming* which sophisticated critics often put down as a "feel good" movie. As stated in the previous chapter, I've also seen *The Sound of Music* at least eight times and plan to watch it again.

Neither movie is very realistic, and I know that several recent films have made positive moral points or lifted our spirits while also including some profanity or showing more skin than they needed to show.

Many old movies frequently offered stereotypes of women, Native Americans, Japanese people, and African Americans which were distortions or greatly laced with prejudice. Women always had to be rescued. American Indians were "savages." The Japanese in World War II films were sadistic, and African Americans were portrayed as passive appendages to the mainstream of American life. Modern movies have challenged these stereotypes even as they have embraced excessive sex and violence in order to sell tickets.

Movies are not the only place, however, in which people of my generation feel cultural shock. Recently trapped in the back seat of someone else's car for two hours, I was treated to the top ten songs as heralded by a local disk jockey. My private reaction was clear: If these are the top ten, may the Lord spare me from the bottom ten!

One of the songs celebrated having sex on an elevator. I think another was a rap song performed by, possibly, two dogs in heat. All of them were played at a volume slightly louder than the eruption of Vesuvius. If hard rock music died tomorrow, it would take weeks for the sound to fade away.

Again, let's try to be fair. Its not easy to be fair, having cultivated certain artistic prejudices throughout my adult life. Popular music has some merits. For example, with rock music, if acoustics are bad, it makes no difference. And were there no musical accompaniment, people dancing to rap music would be arrested for lewd behavior.

I guess that wasn't really very fair. Let me try again. The music of my growing-up years was not always classical. To this day when I hear the *William Tell Overture*, I think of the Lone Ranger. But some of the folk music sung to guitars was pleasant to listen to, even though the performers seemed to sing through their noses by ear. Folk music often made an important statement about civil rights or injustice, even though the rest of it was routine—stuff about boys and girls falling in love.

So what, Mullen, if your generation doesn't like contemporary music or movies? You didn't like Lawrence Welk even though your mother did.

The key difference is that earlier generations didn't look to movie stars and their movies, musicians and their music for role models and norms for living. Music and the movies were on the periphery of life, not in the center. They were appreciated or even admired as entertainers, but we didn't expect them to provide us with guidelines for living. When Ingrid Bergman left her husband to marry the man who was the father of her soon-to-be-born child, it shocked us. It disappointed us. Not so today. It is commonplace.

Rock singers are so openly money-hungry, it boggles the mind. They might as well have become television evangelists. Yet the magazines and papers which celebrate celebrities are regularly encouraging a hedonistic philosophy of life, and millions read them more regularly than the Bible.

So, gentle reader, you can see I've fallen into the trap my generation often does. I've begun to rant. I've begun to rail against the spiritual poverty of our times as shown in movies and music. I fit the stereotype of an old coot who's too old to dance fast and too obtuse to get the deeper meaning of modern music.

You're right. I have been ranting, and I feel better as a result. My sinuses are clear, and I feel morally purer than before I started. But let's wait and see which music survives and which movies are watched thirty years later. As distorted as our cultural voices can become, we know that, over time, music and movies fade from prominence. That which is irrelevant and indecent eventually dies. Those singers who are long on hair and short on talent will come and go.

So, armed with ear plugs and carefully screening the offerings of our local video store, those of us shocked by the culture can shut out the indecently loud and select the best from the rest. And for most of us, there is always *The Sound of Music.*

19

Present Shock

"The world of today...is as different from the world in which I was born as that world was from Julius Caesar's." (Kenneth Boulding)

He's right. Those of us sixty and older have lived through rapid, mind-boggling changes. Some are insignificant. Many, however, intimidate me, and I often feel like a babe in computer toyland.

Where technological change pushes me into a state of mental numbness is in the common events of life—when high tech causes low morale. For example, I was among a group of generationally mature people who were given Christmas music on compact disks. It was a thoughtful gift, but none of us owned a compact disk player. Our entertainment center was state of the art in 1964, but plays only phonograph records, so the state of our art is out of date.

Is it because of my age that I don't enjoy making a telephone call only to get a recorded, disembodied voice punctuated by clicks and beeps? I recently attempted to schedule an appointment with one of the doctors I'm supporting. To do so required a long distance call which was answered by a recorded voice. The voice instructed me to punch a number on the touch-tone phone, depending on which doctor I wanted to see. However, to schedule an appointment (ah hah! At last), I needed to punch a different number.

I did as I was told. However, rather than be connected to a person who could schedule an appointment, I was told by a new voice "I'm not available to talk right now, but if you'll leave a message after the beep, I'll return your call as soon as I can." (Translation: Sometime this century!) The voice continued: "If you need immediate attention, press one." You guessed it. I was brought full circle to the recording which had answered the phone in the first place!

Or consider fax machines. They obviously increase the speed of doing business, and they have many advantages over other kinds of communication. When used to send personal messages, however, fax to fax is worse than face to face. One message arrived on our office machine and was introduced by the words "personal and confidential." Sure.

Computers account for much of our present shock. My fear of computers is documented elsewhere, much to the embarrassment of my children, who use them in their work and swear by them—oops, affirm them.

Even so, hear me out. How do you, gentle reader, respond to the avalanche of computer-generated mail which pretends to be personal, intimate, and deeply concerned about us as individuals? When we, addressed by name, learn that we're finalists in a contest to the win millions in the Publishers Clearing House sweepstakes, do we tingle with excitement? Dare I go out and make a down payment on a yacht?

On those frequent occasions when a computer makes a billing error and efforts to correct it seem fruitless because it is a COMPUTER MISTAKE, do you long for the days when you could call a live human being on the phone and fix the problem? When the bank teller can't tell you your fund balance because the COMPUTER IS DOWN, does your heart overflow with forgiveness toward a machine miles away that cares not whether your creditors will soon be garnisheeing your wages?

While I am mostly alone in this concern (Note: I am the *only* member of the faculty who does not use a computer), others sometimes share my fears. Consider these comments from Ellen Goodman, a nationally syndicated columnist, who bought a television set with several technological features:

> Consider the television which entered our bedroom after its twenty-year-old predecessor rained Technicolor snow down upon Frasier's Seattle and collapsed. The "feature" that we wanted was a set of cordless headphones—otherwise known as the Marriage Saving Component—to allow one of us to read or sleep while the other (who shall remain nameless) watched various large men pursuing various shaped balls across various shaped playing fields.
>
> For reasons too arcane to mention, having to do with cable companies and astrological signs, the only television set that met this requirement came with the following features: a picture within a picture, wraparound sound, a clock, a timer, an on-screen menu, a channel caption guide, a remote control that could run a 747 and a price tag roughly the equivalent of the one on my first car.
>
> Six months later, I have yet to figure out how—let alone why—to watch two pictures at once. The television sits there in mute (or wraparound stereo) disapproval. It's added to the queasy, guilty sensation, utterly unknown to my grandparents, that I am not measuring up to my own possessions.[1]

Our culture tries to have it both ways. It values efficiency, speed, and easy access to information. Computers, voice mail, fax machines, and VCRs do these well. Our culture also *claims* to value individual persons. So technology *simulates* warmth, even intimacy. But like oil and water, technology and intimacy are incompatible. *Simulating* intimacy is like eating a tofu burger and calling it meat.

Most of us—not just old coots like me—dismiss out of hand computer-generated personal messages. We rejoice that secretaries work more efficiently because of computers, fax machines, and CD ROM accessories—whatever they are. But to be wary of technology is not simply to be flotsam on the sea of change.

The enemy is not technology but depersonalization. People in work places who by the hour stare at screens and click keys until carpel tunnel syndrome occurs need to take breaks and converse about children and the meaning of life. Taking time to write a letter by hand is a small step for humanity.

God help us if one day we fax sympathy notes or confess sins by voice mail. Meeting and relating to the persons in places like churches and youth groups is a better way to find a companion than a computer dating service. (Imagine! MACM seeks MACW who shares VBFP. Translation: Middle-aged Christian man seeks middle-aged Christian woman who shares values, beliefs, and fondness for pizza.)

Simulated humanity is a contradiction in terms. After all, God loved the world enough to the send a Human Being to save us, a Real Person who felt joy and sorrow and called us His friends. That Word does, indeed, compute.

20

Real Men Weep

One of the first funeral sermons I preached when I was a young pastor was for an elderly man named Marion Jefferies. Marion was a good kind man who had been particularly good and kind to me my initial year as a rookie preacher. He had both eldered and counseled me, and I admired his forthright and friendly attitude. Nancy and I had eaten with Marion and Oneita several times, and Marion always began the meal with a devotional reading and prayer. It was obvious, too, that this was how they usually did it. They weren't trying to impress the pastor.

So when Marion died of a heart attack while he was attending a church meeting, I was determined to honor this fine man who had been a lifelong faithful servant of God and a helpful father-figure to me. He was much loved, and I worked hours on the sermon, trying to put into words the feelings of the community and celebrate his going home to God.

The Meetinghouse (that's what Quakers call their church buildings) was packed. We shared a hymn, and I read scripture, including the twenty-third Psalm which Marion loved. Four sentences into the sermon I choked up and wept openly. I struggled for composure, but I kept filling up with tears and my voice quavered and sounded like a radio wracked by static. The sermon that I had wanted so much to be a tribute to a man I admired and loved and a source of comfort to his widow, family, and friends turned out to be an embarrassment.

As I spoke to Marion's family and other attenders at the funeral, I apologized for having lost control of my emotions and asked forgiveness. Their reaction was one I will cherish the rest of my life.

"Tom," one man said, his own eyes filled with tears, "you simply did what the rest of us wanted to do." They felt Marion had been honored. They had been given permission to cry. From that moment on, so had I.

Americans in general and men in particular pride themselves on being in control of their emotions. When a man in public life breaks into tears, it's a sign of weakness. When a congresswoman cries before an audience, regardless of the circumstances, her tears are evidence that women aren't tough enough to govern.

Wrong. Real men and real women weep. Sam Keen writes in *Fire in the Belly*, "Since boys are taught not to cry, men must learn to weep. After a man passes through arid numbness, he comes to a tangled jungle of grief and unnamed sorrow. The path to a manly heart was through the valley of tears."[2]

One of the gifts of living longer is learning the truth of Keen's insight. Young men and women right out of law school, business school, or even seminary work hard at suppressing grief. Or anger. Or even compassion. To weep is to lose control. To lose control is to become vulnerable.

There is some truth behind the fear. Those who only weep when a crisis occurs are of little help to others. Tears that are not honest, in fact, may do harm. It would have been stupid of me to have concluded, after learning how Marion's family and friends reacted, "Hey, I must learn to weep at some point in every funeral sermon. Let's see.... Right after I read, 'Yea, though I walk through the valley of the shadow of death...' I could let a single tear roll down my cheek and...."

Wrong again. The tears that reach the eye must come from the heart. Then they heal and honor and comfort.

Spiritual maturity, I've come to believe, is largely a matter of becoming more vulnerable. J.B. Phillips says that the world, particularly the world of "macho" men and women, seeks to convince us that the "hard-boiled" are happy because they never let life hurt them. In contrast, Phillips updates the beatitude better known as "blessed are those who mourn" to read as follows: "Happy are they who bear their share of the world's pain: in the long run they will know more happiness than those who avoid it." [3]

When men and women are able to become their *real* selves, they are less greedy, competitive, and self-loving. As we age, changing circumstances allow spiritual growth to occur. We learn to live with our limitations, so there is less reason to blame others for our deficiencies. We have more history on which to reflect, and we become more aware of our spiritual poverty. We learn, from experience, the reality of temptation, so we can become better forgivers ourselves.

Living longer makes it easier to weep because we know what it means to be vulnerable. We've been afraid often enough, sorrowful on enough occasions, or just come to the point wherein we no longer care if others equate tears with weakness.

Jim Newby, my colleague at Earlham School of Religion, describes his experience this way: "My father died when I was 36 years old. This was the first occasion I can remember when I shed tears as a man. It was the first time that my wife of fifteen years and my daughter who was thirteen years old had ever seen their husband and father cry. With the death of the father, there is the corresponding death of the son, and from this moment on I knew that life would not look the same as it had looked before December 9, 1985. Also, the tears would begin to flow more easily now."[4]

Women are not as trapped by societal expectations as men. They're allowed, indeed expected, to be tender, nurturing, and compassionate. As men grow older, we learn to give ourselves permission to weep, to forgive, to reach out with arms of compassion.

Women are not as trapped by societal expectations as men. They're allowed, indeed expected, to be tender, nurturing, and compassionate. As men grow older, we learn to give ourselves permission to weep, to forgive, to reach out with arms of compassion. That's been true in this man's life, and the only question that remains is this: Why do we have to grow old to get free from the belief that real men are in control of emotions, tough instead of tender-hearted, or aggressive in relationships?

Jesus was a real man. He wept. So can we.

NOTES
1. Ellen Goodman, "Smart Appliances, Foolish Owner," *The Boston Globe*, December 5, 1995.
2. Sam Keen, *Fire in the Belly*, Bantam Books, New York, 1991, p. 135.
3. J.B. Phillips, *Your God Is Too Small*, The Macmillian Company, New

Stuck on the prayer line to Heaven
"Hi! You've reached 1-800-CREATOR. Sorry I can't take your prayer right now, but if you leave your name, number & a short message I'll get right back to you. Have a great day!"

Part V

Free at Last

The waiting room of a doctor's office is well-named. What we do is wait. Several years ago, having gone to the doctor for an annual physical, I waited across from a man who seemed deeply depressed. His face was glum, and he occasionally breathed a sigh.

I thought he had a serious, possibly terminal, health problem. As the days passed (so it seemed), I eventually struck up a conversation with him. I said: "You appear very depressed. I'm a minister. Is there anything I can do to help?"

He exhaled another sigh and shared his story. He was there for the same reason I was—to get his annual physical. Then he said he had just retired from the company where he had labored over forty years and it occurred to him that it was the first time in all those years he'd gotten his physical on his own time. Always before he d gone to the doctor on company time. With a grimace, he concluded: "I find spending my own time in a doctor's office to be terribly depressing!"

Many men and women work hard all their lives so they can retire. They'll finally be free from bosses, drudgery, and obligations. They'll have time to do what they want to do. Instead, they discover new claims on their time and energy, and more than one retiree has uttered a vocational blasphemy: "I wish I were working again."

Many of us have identified our value as persons by our work, and we have difficulty with leisure time. To spend large segments of time relaxing or sight-seeing is to violate the Puritan work ethic. It is to "waste time" in the sense that leisure does not usually produce a product. Nancy and I had a preview of retirement when we took a once-in-a-lifetime dream vacation. It was memorable, but neither of us can imagine being on vacation all the time. Still, aging forces us to ask: How will we spend our time?

Growing older also forces us to consider another question: How best to deal with our estate? Even calling what we own an "estate" sounds odd, as if we were talking about somebody else who is rich. When we sat down and talked about our "last will and testament," it was revealing of what we really valued.

Aging causes us to think about two other aspects of life that we postpone as long as we can: debilitating illness and, eventually, our own deaths. People of faith are supposed to be able to handle these realities with courage and serenity. While leading a workshop for care givers of Alzheimer's victims, I learned that it is possible to rejoice and give thanks in the face of a disease that strips the ones you love of dignity. Privately, we hope our loved ones can be spared the burden of caring for us if we're disabled.

The irony is that after the workshop and before I sat down to finish this book, Nancy had to have her leg amputated and I discovered I have Crohn's disease. Neither of us feels "disabled," however, even though it is not always easy to live each day with patience and good humor.

Death, of course, becomes a closer acquaintance when we grow older. The Christian faith provides enormous resources as we face our own death or the loss of a loved one. Having learned how to weep, we also learn that we grieve—but not without hope. That's why it makes sense to plan the kind of funeral or memorial service we d like to have.

I want mine to have similarities to a party. I want some tears and sadness, but having a family that adores me, warts and all, guarantees that mourning will occur. If my brother Frank is able to attend, I hope he won't give a long prayer. He did that at my ordination service while a dozen people were pressing down on my head and back. It was a beastly hot night, and I was wearing a wool suit. I wondered then if I would survive my brother's prayer. If he gave a prayer as long as that one at my memorial service, it could take all the fun out of it.

The fact is, of course, that we can't control how we die or that all our wishes will be granted. What we can do, while still having some semblance of a sound mind, is affirm what we believe to be true about life—even as we slide towards death.

Wouldn't you know, the words that say it best for me were written by someone else who is anonymous:

Risk

To laugh is to risk appearing the fool.
To weep is to risk appearing sentimental.
To reach out for another is to risk involvement.
To expose feelings is to risk exposing your true self.
To place your ideas, your dreams before a crowd is to risk their loss.
To love is to risk not being loved in return.
To live is to risk dying.
To hope is to risk failure.

But risks must be taken.
Because the greatest hazard in life is to risk nothing.
If we risk nothing and do nothing, we dull our spirits.
We may avoid suffering and sorrow,
But we cannot learn, feel, change, grow, love and live.

Chained by our attitude, we are slaves.
We have forfeited our freedom.
Only if we risk are we free.

The Christian faith offers us freedom while we're alive and freedom after we die. It makes the journey of life worthwhile. One day we are free at last. Great God Almighty, we're free at last.

21

The Mother of All Vacations

In honor of our sixtieth birthdays, our four children and my brother sent us to Hawaii for two weeks. Unlike most of our family holidays, this one was for the sake of pure enjoyment—no speeches, no retreats, no workshops. This trip was to be the Mother of all vacations, the one we'd recall years later while sitting on a nursing home porch unable to remember what we had for breakfast.

So we went openly and unapologetically, as tourists, cameras ready and armed with travelers checks and guidebooks. Tourists usually want to go places where there are no tourists, but it can't be done in Hawaii. Its main industry is tourism, and the islands are luxurious with tropical plants and outstretched palms. We soon learned that we needed half as much luggage and twice as much money. In Hawaii, people don't take vacations. Vacations take people.

On Oahu we stayed in pleasant quarters provided by Honolulu Friends Meeting. However, on the other three islands we visited, we stayed in hotels—luxurious, expensive, well-appointed hotels. In one of them, which was located a few feet from the ocean, we could see the sun set and hear the waves crash against the shore. That hotel provided swimming pools since those crashing waves discouraged frolicking in the ocean. One pool was filled with salt water for those who wanted to feel as if they were in the Pacific. Another pool was filled with fresh water for those who preferred salt-free swimming. A third pool was kept empty for those who couldn't swim. (I made that up.)

Having hung out with Quakers most of our adult lives, we had difficulty adjusting to the luxury expensive hotels provide. A lifetime of sleeping in college dormitories and eating granola at Quaker conferences did not prepare us to stay awhile among the rich and bankrupt. Our condominium on Hawaii (the Big Island, as we veteran travelers say) provided fresh bars of soap each day, matchbooks even though we stayed in nonsmoking suites, and a variety of shampoos and lotions—some of which we used and all of which we brought home. Our luggage, by the time we departed, smelled better than we did.

There is no limit to adventures tourists can choose in Hawaii, especially if your name is Donald Trump. We rented cars which freed us to enjoy the gorgeous scenery for which the islands are deservedly famous. Renting cars is a primary source of income for the entire state, especially if one yields to the pressure to "upgrade" and buy enough insurance to cover any eventuality, including the End of the World. But we drove to the very edge of an active volcano and felt its heat floating up from the ground on which we stood. We were free to stop and visit the many beaches that take your breath away, both when you view them from a distance and when you attempt to swim against the tide.

The beaches were packed with people of many races, nationalities, and sexual orientations. Warned that the Hawaiian sun burns without mercy, we dutifully smeared our bodies with enough lotion to be protected from either an atomic blast or volcanic eruption.

Lying on beaches is a major pastime on the Islands. Being tourists, we visited Wakiki Beach, probably the most famous stretch of sand in the world. Literally thousands of folks were trying to get suntans at premium prices. Anything resembling modesty was conspicuous by its absence. Flesh was everywhere on display, and both males and females seemed totally unselfconscious abut wearing nearly nothing. Some suits were so skimpy I couldn't tell whether those wearing them were inside trying to get out or outside trying to get in. An unofficial contest seemed to be going on to see who could get tanned over the largest percentage of his or her body. Many sat in grotesque positions holding aluminum reflectors to tan spots hard for the sun to reach.. I saw one man lying on his back with his mouth open. Evidently, he was going to win the tanning contest by the skin of his teeth.

For a Midwestern boy who wore boxer trunks to the knees long before basketball players made them stylish, that much flesh caused culture shock. Having been brought up in a conservative home to think that looking at exposed skin would cause blindness, Wakiki Beach posed a moral dilemma for me. To look or not to look was the question. After some meditation, I decided to risk one eye.

We took two helicopter trips, one on Maui and another on Kawai. They were an expensive but excellent means for seeing the beauty of volcanic mountains, dozens of waterfalls, lush tropical forests, and extensive landfills for tourist trash. One of our pilots enjoyed banking his aircraft at sharp angles for better camera vistas. Such quick changes of direction in a fragile aircraft helped explain why every passenger was equipped with seatbelts and paper bags.

Nancy and I took a cruise off Maui sponsored by Greenpeace to view the whales. We spent an afternoon with a boatload of folks who came to photograph these extraordinary creatures and drink large quantities of beer. Large and small whales appeared as if on cue to blow streams of water into the air or suddenly submerge with huge tails thrashing. We also dropped anchor near a small island where an abundance of exotic fish and eels reside. A set of stairs was lowered into the ocean, and all who wished to go snorkeling and observe the fish close up did so. Since I tend to sink in deep water, I watched from the boat. However, my sixty-year-old wife leapt fearlessly into the water and snorkeled up a storm while I explained to the two others remaining on board that I stayed behind to get pictures.

It was the shortest two weeks of our lives. This once-in-a-lifetime trip left us speechless—until we got home and began boring our friends with more details than they cared to learn. A vacation is like love—anticipated with pleasure, experienced as reality, and remembered with nostalgia.

We found we weren't quite able to get free from our inhibitions nor stop worrying about the cost—even though our family had paid the way. The best part of the trip was taking it together, and the good news is that we don't have to fly thousands of miles to watch sunsets side by side, or smell the flowers, or greet each day with an embrace. The blessing of the trip was sharing it with your favorite person. Except, of course, when she went snorkeling alone.

22

An Attitude of Gratitude

Everybody wants to live a long time, but nobody wants to get old. Alternatives to growing older, however, are sobering, so it's best not to rush the aging process but accept it. To some extent we can plan for it. And when we pass sixty we reap certain benefits that otherwise are not available to us.

While there is not much future in being old, it's also true that we are seldom bothered by insurance salesmen. Indeed, their wish for us to live long and well is undoubtedly sincere.

And we are granted more latitude for our personality quirks. By the time we're old enough not to care what anyone says about us, nobody says anything. Age provides some margin for being eccentric.

Civilized young people are usually kind to their elders. They listen to our advice without taking it and laugh at our stories without believing them. They notice our increasing frailty and are good enough to lie about it to us. As one pundit said: "The three ages of people are youth, middle age, and my, but you're looking well!"

The reality of growing older that can be a mixed blessing is retirement. Some people work a lifetime at jobs they hate and persevere in doing their work only because of mortgage payments and the fact their kids teeth didn't come in straight. For them, not going to a daily grind is a reward for survival.

Even so, among this group, retirement often disappoints. Some work harder at loafing than they used to loaf at working. Spouses discover that they had married for better or worse but not for lunch. Retired people have to drink coffee on their own time. When the moment finally arrives when people can do anything they wish, they wish they could do something else.

If sufficient income is available to live comfortably, retirement is still the period in life when we stop quoting the proverb, "Time is money." If that proverb were true, retired people would have more money than they need. Thus, careful financial planning for retirement is a gift to our children. It's good stewardship to be a burden neither to our children or the government.

At this writing I am almost but not yet retired. If we live simply and occasionally beg on street corners, Nancy and I will get along fine. What worries this product of the Puritan work ethic is the open-endedness of retirement. As an observer of re-tired people, it seems they never do all the stuff they intended to do when they didn't have the time.

Wasting time was a cardinal sin in my boyhood home, and I carry those feelings to this day. I understand that time does not always have to be productive in the traditional sense. Reading books, enjoying music, playing with grandchildren, and watching sunsets are worth doing. Robert Fulghum reminds us that almost no one ever wishes he or she had spent more time at the office. Experiencing life is its own excuse for being.

But simply filling time, I've been taught, is wasteful. Before any of us retires, we should be required to sit at home for a week and watch daytime television. This is a foolproof recipe for wast-ing time. The fear I bring as retirement draws near is that I will wake up in the morning with nothing useful to do and go to bed at night with it still to be done.

Those who model a happy retirement meet two criteria: They have something to live on and much to live for. With or without grandchildren, happily retired people stay connected to the world. One woman in her nineties, a member of our congregation, was a social activist all her life. She had worked among Native Americans in her early years, and she never lost her drive for peace and justice in the world. In the last year of her life she sometimes called on the phone to urge me to write a legislator or attend a rally or donate to a cause. Her life had meaning.

Retired people I admire take care of themselves. They run. They walk. They swim. I'm married to such a person. Nancy insists we eat nutritional meals. Her desire to be fitted with a prosthesis is partly so she can return to her regular exercise program.

I sometimes cheat on my diet because I refuse to let my pancreas totally run my life, but care of the body is a form of stewardship. When old people get together, they often talk about their health—their "organ recital" as the joke says. They'll be able to talk about it longer if they eat, sleep, and exercise well. One friend, long retired, said you could always tell which folks took care of themselves in a retirement community. "Some," he said, "were canes and some were ables."

Mostly, a happy retirement is a matter of attitude. Thomas Carlyle wrote, "Our grand business in life is not to see what lies dimly at a distance, but to do what lies clearly at hand." People don't get cynical or bitter or grouchy simply because they are old. They probably have had those attitudes for many years. An attitude of gratitude invests life with purpose and joy at age thirty, or earlier, and it continues to do so at age sixty, or longer.

In a little while I'll know whether I'll be able to match the grace, purpose, and joy of those who are role models for retirement. Certainly there is work to be done, and I've managed to transcend mediocre health for years. I have grandchildren who love me. Enthusiasm for life during retirement is a genuine option. I wish it for myself and all others facing retiring years. Years wrinkle the skin, but a lack of enthusiasm for life wrinkles the soul.

23

Where There's a Will

"Tom, it's time we re-did our wills," Nancy announced one evening at the very moment my Indiana Hoosiers were tied for the lead with two minutes left to play. She knows that I will agree to deal with that issue right after the game. In fact, she knows that I will agree to deal with any issue so long as it's *after* the game.

I was trapped. I've resisted talking about estate plans for years, partly because it's much ado over very little and partly because I don't want to face the hard decisions wills force us to make. Being of sound mind, I'd just as soon avoid the whole issue.

The other impetus, in addition to spousal pressure, is the reality of taxes. Where there's a will, there's an inheritance tax that can be less or more, depending on the choices we make. And while I regard myself as a loyal American, the thought of the government receiving more of my estate than is absolutely necessary provides a major incentive for hiring a lawyer—and writing one's will carefully.

We began by talking in general about what is going to be left after we're gone. The discussion surprised us because we realized we're worth more than we thought. Take our house, for example. It is an old house with a damp basement that has never been featured in the annual Richmond parade of homes. Having lived there for thirty years, the mortgage has been paid. Be there ever so many payments, there's finally no place like home.

We've been through a lot with this old house. Nothing makes your home feel more like a castle than getting an estimate for repairing the roof. "House-broke" can refer to families as well as pets. As Nancy and I considered what to do with the house in our estate planning, we realized how far we had come. It was possible to sit in any room, turn completely around, and not see something to fix.

We discovered we had no good idea as to what it was worth. We also found that we cared little about its monetary value and lots about how the next owners would view it. Would they change everything? Would they appreciate the fact that nine generations of students had sat cross-legged on the floor, debating the meaning of life while messing pizza toppings in the rug? Would they care that all our children and grandchildren had learned peek-a-boo in the living room? Or that we held hands around the table while our grandson blessed the food, the dog, the gerbils, every family member by name, his friends at school, and the tables and chairs? An old, inexpensive house holds as much happiness as a new, costly one, so we deferred any decision about what to do with the house in our will. Nancy and I had never found any decision too big in life to avoid.

"Let's do the liquid assets by percentages," my wife suggested. That ought to be easy enough.

It should have been. We didn't have to know how many dollars would be left in order to decide on the percentage for each recipient. Ten percent here, five percent there. What could be simpler?

But how do we decide on the precise percentage? We have four children. Some of them have children. Some don't. The Meeting of which we've been a part as long as we'd lived in Richmond is important to us, too. And so are Earlham, the School of Religion, and a host of charities—everything from the Friends World Committee to the Oceanic Society (save the oceans) to Defenders of Wildlife (save the wildlife) to the Wilderness Society (save the wilderness for the wildlife.)

We imagined how excited a charity might be when its trustees received word that they would be receiving a bequest from the estate of Tom and Nancy Mullen. And how less-excited they would later be when it amounted to enough money to pay for coffee breaks for a year if they didn't use cream.

Writing a will forced us to decide which recipients could best use the money and property we'd leave behind. Our cottage on a lake, where Nancy and I had spent many hours working jigsaw puzzles while waiting for our teenagers to return with the car, is cherished by all four children. So leave it to all four of them, right? But it's geographically accessible only to three, so fairness becomes an issue. And which ones will tend to it each year, mow the grass, and take the pipes apart so they won't freeze over the winter?

We decided to think about the cottage another time. So after two solid hours of philosophizing about writing a will, we'd managed to defer some decisions, postpone others, and seek counsel on the rest. Sometime soon, of course, we'll really have to do this task, or let nature and the tax collector do it for us.

The exercise, albeit aborted, was useful. We discovered that what we owned was not nearly so important as the values we held. Having less to bequeath than Donald Trump also meant that our chances of people being sad rather than happy when we died were increased. Jesus was right when he said that treasures in heaven were more valuable than earthly ones. They give meaning to one's life, and the IRS can't touch them. Hallelujah!

24

Letting Go

The topic was familiar but the group was special. I had been asked to lead a workshop on humor and faith for a group of caregivers to Alzheimer's patients. A few of them were professionals—nurses, administrators, counselors—but most were family members—spouses, children, siblings.

Unknown to them was the fact that I came with considerable anxiety. Probably all of us carry certain fears about health. We hope we'll be spared cancer, heart disease, or Alzheimer's. Publicly, I joke that I'd prefer to live to be ninety and then be shot by a jealous husband. Privately, I fear dying by inches, losing the ability to know what's happening around me, and becoming totally dependent on others for my care.

Aging inevitably feeds such fears. We know that, over time, our brain cells wear out and the ability to remember fades. At least, I think that's what happens. More than once I've wondered if my forgetfulness were normal for my age or was I in the early stages of Alzheimer's? Do I have, if not Alzheimer's, "Halfheimer's?"

During the workshop we explored ways humor and laughter enable us to keep life's trials in perspective. The group embraced the idea as if they had been seeking permission to laugh as an antidote to the pain and stress of daily caregiving to loved ones.

Some shared personal guilt they felt when they became resentful about the unpredictable or irritating behavior of their loved ones.

Caring for victims of dementia is, in many ways, harder on the caregiver than the patient. The one with Alzheimer's is not always aware of his or her mental deterioration. Caregivers see how their parents or siblings become disoriented and dependent, and their hearts break. They become protective of the ones for whom they are responsible, and they may resent laughter that seems to be at the expense of a patient's self-esteem.

During the course of the workshop, however, a small miracle occurred. Because nearly all who were there shared common feelings of guilt, anger, or despair, they discovered they could laugh aloud at some of the bizarre behaviors and strange statements their Alzheimer's victims/family members put forth. For outsiders to laugh about such incidents would have been inappropriate. For caregivers, who had, so to speak, paid their dues, remembering with laughter was therapeutic.

I learned that caregivers often share their stories in support groups and newsletters. One hospitalized Alzheimer's patient, prone to wandering, was found near an elevator far from where she was supposed to be. She told an attendant that she was waiting for a bus. The attendant tried to persuade her to return to her room without success. Finally, the attendant said: "You know, Mrs. A., I think the bus company is on strike." The patient replied, "Oh, okay," and went back to her room.

Another story recalled a patient who was convinced a fire was burning under his bed. Nobody could convince him there was no fire. Eventually a nurse took a glass of water from his bedside table, threw the water under the bed, and said: 'There, I put it out." The patient thanked the nurse, rolled over, and went to sleep.

One caregiver from Alabama had taken his father, an Alzheimer's patient, out for a ride. As they drove past a yard that contained dozens of bird houses, the father pointed to them and said: "Look at the...Look at the...." He couldn't remember the word for birdhouse. Then, in a moment of inspiration, exclaimed, "Look at all the feathered condominiums!"

As stories were shared, the caregivers laughed until they cried. A mixture of laughter and tears was appropriate, as joy and sorrow usually come from the same deep place—the affection we feel for loved ones. It was a case of laughing *with*, not laughing *at*. The laughter was contagious and healing.

Workshop leaders are supposed to help groups see things more clearly or discover how a truth connects to them. In this case, the process was reversed. Whatever my fears of one day being an Alzheimer's patient myself, I realized that those who care for victims of dementia can do more than cope and are sometimes able to rejoice and give thanks in the middle of their circumstances. An ability to laugh in the chaos of discouragement witnesses to God's trustworthiness.

I still prefer a fast, clean, and painless end to life. Whatever happens, however, Jesus's promise is comforting. "In the world you have tribulation; but be of good cheer, I have overcome the world." (John 16:33 RSV)

Indeed.

25

Two Funerals
and a Party

After age sixty, we attend a lot of funerals. Some of them, even, are for people younger than we are. In addition to services for relatives, after sixty the natural order prevails, and we attend funerals for favorite teachers, leaders in our churches, and older colleagues.

The older we are, the more aware of death we become. As Artemis Ward said: "Homer is dead, Dante is dead, Shakespeare is dead, and I'm not feeling so well myself." Aging emphasizes our mortality, but a funeral reminds us that when we stop getting older, we re dead. Providence has placed death at the end of life in order to give us time to prepare for it. Or, if not prepare for it, at least think about it.

I often reflect on what I hope will be true of my own memorial service. Having preached at many funerals and attended countless others, I have strong feelings about how the whole event should be observed. I prefer a memorial service which doesn't require a corpse to be present and allows time for the initial shock to be absorbed.

Most of us hope a large crowd will show up, although attendance at funerals, even of famous people, depends mostly on the weather. We also hope that some of those who come will be sad, illustrated by the man who resolutely carried no life insurance because he wanted no one to be glad he had died.

Memorial services are communal events. They are times of mourning but also celebrating. When my teacher, Elton Trueblood, died, many persons spoke out of the silence about his ninety-four years of life. His family, colleagues, students, and friends remembered him in a wide variety of ways—some comments bringing tears, others hearty laughter.

His rich life and ministry made it easy to remember both our loss and moments of joy. His faithfulness reminded all of us that death is not a period, but a comma in the story of life. A funeral is a punctuation mark.

Afterwards, we gathered for refreshments and trading stories and memories. Friendships were renewed. Hugging, laughter, and tears were the emotions of the day. Elton, who loved a good party, would have been pleased.

His memorial service was larger in scope but similar in character to the funeral for my favorite aunt. Only about twenty-five people attended Aunt Helen's service, mostly relatives and members of her church. Like Elton's, her gathering was also full of sadness and happy memories. Her pastor told how Aunt Helen, who had no children of her own, invested her life as a school teacher for other people's sons and daughters. He helped us become, for a few moments, a fellowship of persons gathered because of a common relationship. It felt just right, and afterwards most of the attenders went out to lunch together.

I've presided at some funerals very different from these two. Occasionally, I was asked to participate because the deceased had no church affiliation, and the funeral director invited me to help out the family. Such funerals are seldom communal. They have the quality of a ritual, a respectful and courteous act by a family who seeks to do the proper thing.

For me and my house, I hope the memorial service will be a happy religious event. I want people to sing hymns, and I hope friends will recall some happy moments. If they don't, much of my life will have been wasted. The service shouldn't go on too long, as refreshments will be served afterwards and common to Christians is a love of eating. A memorial service reminds us that, at death, we leave behind all that we have but celebrate all that we are. Without defining what a really good life is, at least we can say it is one so full that even the funeral director is sorry to see us go.

What is said at a funeral should be reasonably honest. Grief has a way of clouding our memories, and some services leave the impression that mean and useless people never die. This much is true: Perfect people never die, and when we gather to remember someone, telling the truth helps the healing. Once I heard a daughter, while speaking at her father's memorial service, say this: "He was often hard to live with and, at times, a real grouch. But he was my Dad, and I loved him."

When I go, if someone remembers me as patient, a case of mistaken identity has occurred. I pray, but no one who knows me would confuse me with St. Francis of Assisi.

Being remembered as we really were and still loved frees mourners from vague feelings of guilt. God's Grace is what allows us to celebrate the lives of people who die, not our ranking in *Who's Who* or a listing in the most recent volume of *The Best People Who Ever Lived.*

The way American society does funerals invites dishonesty in the form of denial. We say a loved one "has not died but is only asleep for awhile," even though no one ever puts an alarm clock in the casket. When I viewed Aunt Helen the last time, she was wearing her best clothes and lying in a box, wearing her glasses with her eyes closed. Special lighting tried to provide a life-like appearance.

It didn't work. Aunt Helen never slept with her glasses on, or in a box, and never in her best clothes. Our efforts to ease the pain of loss slide into denial. Better to have pictures around that recall real memories. Maybe it's my own problem, but I don't want a skilled mortician to help me look better than I looked when I was alive.

In short, when we die, it's best to let our lives speak for themselves, and religious "spin doctors" only delay real feelings. If we are fortunate enough to be part of a faith community, words of resurrection and hope can be embraced and claimed. We can laugh together and weep together because the joke is ultimately on the Grim Reaper. That's why he's so grim.

The final gathering can be a party. As I think about death—as lots of people my age do—this is what I d like: A party, and you are all invited. Refreshments will be served.

"Mom we need more punch! You never should
have agreed to this funeral party idea."